Understand Philosophy of Mind

D0288127

Teach®
Yourself

Understand Philosophy of Mind

Mel Thompson

Hodder Education

338 Euston Road, London NW1 3BH

Hodder Education is an Hachette UK company

First published in UK 2003 by Hodder Education

First published in US 2003 by The McGraw-Hill Companies, Inc.

This edition published 2012

British Library Cataloguing in Publication Data: a catalogue record
for this title is available from the British Library.

Library of Congress Catalog Card Number: on file.

10 9 8 7 6 5 4 3 2 1

The publisher has used its best endeavours to ensure that any
website addresses referred to in this book are correct and active at
the time of going to press. However, the publisher and the author
have no responsibility for the websites and can make no guarantee
that a site will remain live or that the content will remain relevant,
decent or appropriate.

The publisher has made every effort to mark as such all words
which it believes to be trademarks. The publisher should also
like to make it clear that the presence of a word in the book,
whether marked or unmarked, in no way affects its legal status as
a trademark.

Every reasonable effort has been made by the publisher to trace the
copyright holders of material in this book. Any errors or omissions
should be notified in writing to the publisher, who will endeavour
to rectify the situation for any reprints and future editions.

Hachette UK's policy is to use papers that are natural, renewable
and recyclable products and made from wood grown in sustainable
forests. The logging and manufacturing processes are expected to
conform to the environmental regulations of the country of origin.

www.hoddereducation.co.uk

Cover image © Justimagine – Fotolia

Typeset by Cenveo Publisher Services

Printed in Great Britain by CPI Cox & Wyman, Reading

Also available
in ebook

Contents

Meet the author

Could you ever meet this author? We have to assume that, if you read this book, you will know something of what I think – at least to the extent that I offer personal comments on the ideas I describe – and that, if you email me with questions or comments (which you are free to do), I will learn something of what you think, and will respond. But what does such a meeting imply? If I am no more than the firing of neurons in my brain, and you in yours, how can we know one another? Would an exchange of brain scans adequately replace a meeting of minds?

Scratch the surface of any aspect of human life, and you will come up with questions that are considered under the general title of the 'philosophy of mind'. I first became interested in philosophical questions because I wanted to make sense of life, to integrate reason and emotions, and to gets to grips with my need for meaning and purpose in life while recognizing the many ways in which life is limited by our circumstances and ultimately by our fragility and mortality.

With billions of neurons and trillions of synaptic connections, our brains are amazingly complex and flexible, and we know that there is an intimate connection between our brains and our consciousness as individual human beings. But how are we to understand that connection? What is it that gives me a sense of being myself? I find such questions fascinating and often bewildering; there is no greater mystery than the human mind, and none more relevant.

I hope you enjoy reading *Understand Philosophy of Mind* and, if you still want to meet 'me', more is revealed on my website, www.mel-thompson.co.uk

Mel Thompson

January 2012

In one minute

Here are some of the questions with which the philosophy of mind is concerned:

▶ What is my mind, and how does it relate to my body?
▶ Are my mind and my brain one and the same thing?
▶ Could a perfect neuroscience tell us all we need to know about the mind?
▶ What is consciousness? Can it be disembodied?
▶ How does the mind know things? Do we passively receive data from the outside world, or does our mind shape the world we experience?
▶ What does it mean to be an individual? What gives me my identity?
▶ Can I really know another person, or am I just guessing from what I see and hear of them?
▶ Am I free to act, or is freedom an illusion in a totally determined physical world?

Questions about the mind have always been central to philosophy, and particularly the fundamental question about the relationship between mind and body. There is a whole spectrum of views on this, ranging from a dualism that sees mind as separate from and potentially independent of the body, to a materialist view that identifies the mind with neural activity.

It is difficult to imagine a question more immediate or relevant than this. Social life, morality and basic self-respect all depend on our common-sense notion of ourselves as free, conscious, intelligent and responsible individuals. Aided by memory and our ability to communicate with other people, we have a sense of who we are; we have a point of view; we can become the subject of biography. Yet neuroscience appears to reduce the mind to neural activity in the brain, processing inputs from the senses and organizing physical responses to them in a causally conditioned physical chain of events that leaves no scope for a guiding self or mind.

The philosophy of mind explores who we are, and does so today against the background of a developing neuroscience that appears to challenge all our assumptions about what it means to be a thinking, feeling, acting human being. However, we shall see that our knowledge of the way in which the brain works shows that it is far more flexible and responsive than we had imagined. Our lifestyle and habitual actions shape the neural pathways in our brain, so we are far from being simply a product of neural activity.

In exploring these questions, the philosophy of mind both sharpens our views about ourselves, and helps us to assess the nature and limits of what science can show.

Introduction

'Who am I?' is the most fundamental question that anyone can ask.

There are many superficial answers to it, but few are satisfactory. I have a name, but what does that mean? I can change my name, without changing myself. I have friends and relatives, a career, a position in society; I am 'known' to a good number of people, who rely on me and predict how I will act. But if I live simply in order to fulfil their expectations, is that authentic living? Am I no more than a product of what others expect? Could I go against everything that others have come to know about me, and do something completely out of character and outrageous? Am I, even for a moment, really free to do whatever I like?

And does anyone else know the real me, anyway? They may guess what I am thinking, but they cannot actually know what goes on in my mind. Their idea of me is put together from what they have observed and what I have said. But that's hardly certain knowledge: I could be an actor, fooling them all. And if they do not know the real me, can I ever fully know anyone else? Am I alone in this world, except for what I can guess about other people?

When a relationship breaks down, or a friend does something completely out of character, we find it profoundly disturbing, because we tend to rely on other people. We assume we know them and can trust them to act in a reasonably predictable way. We take for granted the fact that they have minds and personalities; that they can be known, loved, feared or detested. But how – and to what extent – can we ever 'know' another person?

And what is a 'person', anyway? Am I simply a complex body, controlled by patterns of electrochemical impulses in my brain? If so, do I change as my body changes? How can I possibly be the same 'person' from babyhood to old age? If alcohol, drugs, a severe blow to the head or a degenerative disease can change my personality, warping or destroying the 'mind' that has been known to other people, then am I really just a by-product of a physical body? Am I fooling myself that I am in control of things when, in reality, I am simply a small and totally predictable part of the physical order?

And what does it mean to be conscious? Are animals conscious? They certainly appear to be, but does that give them a 'mind' like our own? And if so, should we be killing and eating them, or trying to communicate with them?

And what of computers? Is the brain sufficiently like a computer that, fed with an appropriately elaborate program, or the ability to learn for itself, a sufficiently powerful computer could actually become intelligent? Become a 'person' even? Perhaps machines have a primitive intelligence already. But, if so, what do we mean by intelligence?

Prevailing views in the philosophy of mind are always shifting. Fifty years ago, most philosophers tended to accept some form of dualism, at least to the extent that they considered minds and brains to have very different properties, and regarded behaviourist and reductionist views as inadequate. Today it is materialism that is the fashionable approach in both philosophy and cognitive science, and it is dualism that is attempting a comeback as the limitations of a materialist view are being exposed.

One reason for the importance of the philosophy of mind is that it overlaps with other areas of philosophy – you can't really get to grips with the theory of knowledge without a view on the nature of mind, nor can ethics make sense without a view of the nature of human freedom and responsibility, and the nature of the mind relates closely to the nature of the universe as we perceive it, which raises fundamental questions about the nature of reality.

It is also a branch of philosophy which needs to work alongside other disciplines – medicine, neuroscience and psychology – all three of which make assumptions about the nature of mind. It is all too easy to assume that neuroscience provides the last word, and that we should therefore try to get our ideas about the mind and what it means to be a conscious individual to fit with what it tells us about neural activity. However, it is more challenging and relevant to question and examine the basis on which neuroscience works, assessing what it can and cannot tell us. What sort of information is science able to provide? After all, it is one thing to plot out the chemical and electrical changes in large numbers of neurons, quite another to experience oneself as a conscious and thinking subject. How can these two ways of looking at the mind match up?

The structure of this book

Clearly, the philosophy of mind is an enormous field of study, and a book such as this can do no more than touch on or outline some of the main debates, and point to the questions that need to be addressed.

The first four chapters give a broad historical overview of the issues:

1 From the earliest traditions of Western philosophy, there has been discussion of the nature of the self and the mind. We shall look briefly at ideas about the self in Plato, Aristotle and later Greek thought, but also at the importance of the idea of the self or soul in later medieval thinking. Am I an eternal soul, trapped within the body? Do I have a destiny beyond this world? Both in philosophical and religious terms, vital issues were raised during this period, and many questions were framed that are still discussed today.

2 From the time of Descartes, in the 17th century, the discussion of mind became dominated by his dualistic idea of the mind as an unextended, thinking substance linked to a physical body. Discussions of Descartes and reactions against his thought, with a range of mind/body options spanning materialism, idealism and many different forms of dualism, were the core issue in the philosophy of mind right up to the second half of the 20th century. The debates took in issues of epistemology (the theory of knowledge) and language. How is it possible to know another person's mind? What does it mean to call someone, or some action, intelligent?

3 From the mid-20th century, however, the debates broadened and took into account the growth of computer science, artificial intelligence and the functional approach to the mind. At the same time, linguistics developed as a separate discipline, raising a whole new range of issues about the function of communication and evolutionary psychology sought to understand how and why consciousness has developed and the advantage it gives a species. These disciplines together form a broad category of cognitive science. The key questions of this period were less 'Do we have an immortal soul?' or 'How can we prove the validity of ascribing a mental predicate?' but more 'What does the mind actually *do*? What difference does it make? How does it operate in processing sense experience and making decisions?'

4 More recently, there have been considerable advances in the understanding of the way in which the brain works, particularly since, by means of fMRI (functional magnetic resonance imaging) we are able to observe brain activity in a living human subject. This correlation of mental and neural activities, along with a generally view that everything is physical and that the mind should therefore be understood in physical terms, has shifted both the balance of the debate away from dualism and in favour of some form of physicalist or materialist view of the mind.

The remaining chapters of the book return to some of the key questions in the philosophy of mind, examining them in the light of the thinkers and theories outlined in the first part:

▶ What is the nature of consciousness, and why does it present a 'hard' problem? How is it possible for something physical (the brain) to generate consciousness?
▶ How does our understanding of the nature of mind relate to questions about the theory of knowledge? Does all knowledge come through the senses, or are some ideas innate?
▶ What does it mean to be an individual? Am I the same person now as the baby I once was? How does our personality develop?
▶ Can we know the minds of other people, or can we do no more than guess what they are like from their words and actions?
▶ Are we free to choose how we act, or are we determined by physical and neural causes? If the latter is the case, should we be held morally responsible for what we do?

Finally, we shall consider whether the discussions that take place in the philosophy of mind are adequate to account for the creative aspects of the mind in the arts and religion.

The problem with the philosophy of mind (as with most philosophy) is that, in order to appreciate anything, you need to know something about almost everything. Inevitably, therefore, there will need to be a fair amount of overlap and cross-referencing between the first and second parts of the book.

A warning: Be prepared for some nonsense! Some of the theories and conclusions in the philosophy of mind are what might politely be termed 'counter-intuitive' – in other words, they go against everything that common sense would expect. To say that the physical world is simply a feature of our mind, or that a headache is no more than a disposition to hold one's head, look glum and reach for aspirin, is clearly nonsense. But so is the claim that the rich variety of human experience can be exhaustively described and explained in terms of waves of activity among the billions of neurons that make up our brains. My experience is made possible by neural activity, but it is certainly experience 'of' something quite other than what is happening in the brain's grey folds.

Take it from me, the physical world does exist, and headaches are real enough even if you give no visible indication of your suffering. Philosophers have the infuriating habit of driving arguments to their logical conclusion, even if they appear to have left the realm of sanity in order to do so. But don't give up on them; sometimes the important thing is to follow the logic of an argument, even if its conclusion appears to be less than sensible.

But, above all, remember that you have the ultimate criterion for assessing all such theories; you have a mind. You are using it at this moment. As your eyes are scanning these lines, neurons are firing in your brain and energy is being used, whatever your mind is, it is engaged in interpreting these marks on paper (physical or digital), forming concepts and relating them to a whole network of meanings that you have learned. The ideas themselves are being assessed and related to all that you have experienced in your life so far. And all of this is happening automatically, in what has become a normal mental function – reading. Perhaps, the final question to ask of all theories is this: *Does this make sense of what I experience myself to be?*

1

From the Greeks to the 16th century

In this chapter you will:
- *examine the ideas of Plato and Aristotle on the soul*
- *explore the legacy of ancient Greek philosophy*
- *consider some religious and philosophical views on the self.*

The Greek word that most obviously describes the self or mind is *psyche*, from which, of course, we get the word psychology. But the *psyche* was not exactly what we would call mind, since it was often used in a much wider sense as the power of a living thing to grow and move and have an effect upon its surroundings, as well as to will something to happen, and other aspects of what we would call 'mental states'. Thus, for example, both Plato and Aristotle thought that plants had *psyche*, and the very first philosopher and scientist, Thales of Miletus (6th century BCE), described magnets as having *psyche* because of their power to move other things, and declared that 'all things are full of gods', implying that *psyche* is universal.

Notice therefore that the ancient philosophers looked at mental states without trying to relate them to a separate, immaterial substance called 'mind'. *Psyche* was simply the word used to describe the distinctive features of living things, as opposed to inanimate objects.

The ancients were as much scientists as philosophers. Democritus (b. mid-5th century BCE), who analysed everything in terms of atoms in space, thought that the *psyche* comprised the very simplest of atoms (spherical ones); Heraclitus (540–480 BCE), contemplating the process of change, thought that the *psyche* was a kind of transforming fire. The Pythagoreans (as described by Plato in

Timaeus) thought of the *psyche* as a controlling and balancing principle of harmony within the body.

The ancients were also influenced by the idea of reincarnation. Herodotus knew of the Egyptian idea of an immortal soul being able to leave a body at death and move into another about to be born. Indeed, Pythagoras (*c.*570–497 BCE), who was a notable philosopher as well as a mathematician, held that the souls of those who had died could enter into animals for their future lives.

Insight

The implications of reincarnation for Greek thought are quite profound. If there is a soul (or *psyche*) that can enter into an animal after having been a human, then it cannot be identified *exclusively* with the thinking element of the self – otherwise you would end up with 'thinking' animals. Rather the *psyche* that they thought able to be reincarnated is much broader, comprising the basic power to animate a body and give it character.

In the next chapter we shall consider Descartes' dualism of an unextended, thinking mind and an extended physical body. The *psyche* of the ancient Greeks was far more than that; for the narrower sense of a thinking element, the Greeks would have used the term *nous*. A key question in the philosophy of mind is therefore whether one should be considering 'mind' (in the narrow sense of a thinking self) at all, or rather the broader concept of *psyche*.

An immortal soul?

A good starting point for examining Plato's view of the soul lies with the source of his original inspiration – Socrates. Plato (427–347 BCE) presents Socrates (469–399 BCE) as a thinker who was concerned above all with the question about what it means to live well. In other words, he is concerned with the nature and purpose of a human life – that which raised the human above the animal. When Socrates was condemned, he accepted death calmly, not thinking of himself as limited to his physical body. For Socrates, the self is largely non-physical, and the body is not the true person. His task, shown in his challenge to conventional thought and in his acceptance of death, was to explore the spiritual, or non-material, aspects of human life.

Plato argued for a dualism of immaterial substance (*psyche*) and physical body. In *Timaeus*, he claims that it is an essential feature of the *psyche* to be self-moving, since it is the power to move and change other things, rather than being itself moved by the physical body. The *psyche* is the animating principle, and without it we are left with a corpse. But in the same dialogue he introduces the idea that the relation of soul to body may be likened to the way in while a lyre is tuned – in other words, that the soul is not part of the physical body, but as the arrangement through which the whole body is able to live. Later, in *Phaedo*, Plato was to change his theory somewhat. Instead of seeing the *psyche* as responsible for animating and giving rise to human activity and mental states, he limits the mind to the reasoning part, and leaves emotions and other aspects of human life – like the ability to perceive and respond to something – to the realm of the body. By the time he wrote *The Republic*, however, he saw the *psyche* as more complex, and allowed that it was concerned with all aspects – both those connected with emotion and activity, and those connected with thought.

In *The Republic*, he makes the analogy between the city and the soul. Just as the soul has three parts – reason, the spirited (or seat of passions) and the basic appetites – so the city has its philosopher-rulers or guardians, those who defend it and make it work, and the workers, who seek only the satisfaction of their needs. The self, therefore, for Plato includes, but is not limited to, the reasoning part. He sees the ideal life is one in which all three aspects of the self are balanced. The basic appetites are held in check by the active faculties, which are themselves guided by reason. The good life is achieved through integrity, not elimination. He does not deny the appetites and actions, but places them firmly under the control of reason.

Overall, for Plato, the self has as its goal an understanding of the good and the beautiful, and it is capable of doing this in spite of the hazards, frustrations and limitations of the particular things with which we are surrounded in this life. The impulse - led by reason, but not limited to reason - is to aspire to something higher. Thus, given the choice of seeking truth or pleasure, Plato suggests that we should opt for truth, since pleasure is limited and transient. In an unstable and hazardous world, the mind aspires to understand the good and the beautiful – thus displaying both its origin and its true home.

Plato argues that the *psyche* has knowledge of the 'Forms' (his term of the universals in which particular things participate) rather than simply of the particular things that we see in experience. So, for example, we have a general concept of 'tree' although we have seen only particular trees. But, since he believes that the Forms are eternal, he reasons that the *psyche* must be immortal, having gained knowledge of the Forms before birth. For Plato, there is a real feeling that the self has a come down to earth from its natural heavenly abode, and is entombed within the physical body, but at the same time – through reason and knowledge of the Forms – it cannot help but betray its origins. This is emphasized by a pun that arises in the Greek, for the body (*soma*) becomes the tomb (*sema*) of the soul. Naturally enough, the soul is not at home in this tomb, and aspires to transcend it.

However, Plato's concern for the distinction between soul and body should not lead us to assume that he saw individuals as in some way arriving on earth fully formed. He took the view (e.g. in *The Republic*, Book 6) that people were like plants, developing according to the soil in which they are planted, arguing that the soul takes on the characteristics of its environment. He was also very aware of the ability of society to influence the individual. Clearly, Plato needs to account for the very obvious influence that nurture and environment have on individuals, if he is also to claim that the mind pre-dates the body and is linked with the eternal realm of the Forms.

Making us what we are

Aristotle (384–322 BCE) thought that all living things had souls, and that the *psyche* was a 'principle of life' – that which distinguishes the living from the inanimate. Within the range of creatures having souls, there was a subset, namely those who were also capable of rational thought. Thus the rational mind (for which the Greek term is *nous*) is part of, but not identical with the *psyche*.

Aristotle rejected Plato's idea of the *psyche* as an immaterial substance, but also rejected the Atomists view of it as a fine and extended physical thing, and the Pythagorean approach of seeing it as the agent of balance within the body. The shorthand way of describing Aristotle's view of the soul and its relationship to the body – set out in his book *On the Soul* (*De Anima*) – is to say *that the soul is what makes a thing what it is*. In other words, it is that thing's essence, as he shows in this example:

> 'suppose that the eye were an animal – sight would have been its soul, for sight is the substance, or essence, of the eye... the eye being merely the matter of seeing; when seeing is removed the eye is no longer an eye, except in name.

> 'As the pupil plus the power of sight constitutes the eye, so the soul plus the body constitutes the animal.

> *'From this is indubitably follows that the soul is inseparable from its body, or at any rate that certain parts of it are (if it has parts) – for the actuality of some of them is nothing but the actualities of their bodily parts.'*

Now this suggests that, when we are dealing with the mind, we should not assume that it might in some way be shown as existing in among the various parts into which the body can be divided. However, just because it cannot be in parts of the brain or other physical system does not make it any less a part of the 'essence' of a person.

Aristotle sees the *psyche* as the form that organizes the material body into what it essentially is. Notice that this makes the *psyche* distinct from the material body, but not separate from it. You do not have the body in one place and the soul somewhere else – they are locked together, the former being given its shape and characteristics by the latter. The soul is thus the actuality of the body as an organized thing. Aristotle is therefore able to dismiss the question whether the soul and the body are one. Using his own analogy, it is as meaningless ask this as to ask whether the wax and the shape given to it by the stamp are one. There is no 'shape' without wax that has been pressed into that particular shape. But wax and shape are not therefore identical; they are very different things – the one is matter, the other is the form in which the matter appears.

A statue remains a piece of marble. You cannot separate out the marble from the statue. You cannot point to that which is statue but not marble; and to think that 'statue' must refer to something other than that which the marble forms is nonsense. However, as we shall see later, such nonsense was still being railed against by Gilbert Ryle in the 20th century, in what he termed a 'category mistake', even though Aristotle had dealt with it quite adequately more than two millennia earlier.

....

Insight

From time to time, as you read through the arguments presented in this book, refer back to these quotes from Aristotle. I have a feeling that much time and effort in the philosophy of mind could have been saved had his principles had been attended to more carefully. We shall see later that what he has to say – namely that the soul or mind is distinct from particular material parts of the body, that is it holistic, and that it is inseparable from the body – has implications for much modern discussion about materialism and functionalism. What Aristotle is surely saying here is that the way you describe a soul, or the essence of an animal – human or otherwise – depends on, but is not reducible to, what one might say about parts of that animal body, including (most importantly) its brain.

If he were alive today Aristotle would have been be quick to point out that detailed descriptions of neural activity are simply descriptions of parts of the body and cannot show its essence.

For Aristotle, the self or mind is the essence or form of a human being, an essence that is distinct from but also inseparable from the material body. But we need to distinguish between the 'soul' in the sense of being an independent, living thing (as seen in animals) and the distinctively human ability to think. This distinction is important because much modern debate concerns consciousness, along with sensations, emotions, responses and the like. These are features of life that humans share with animals. On the other hand, the principle form of dualism, stemming from Descartes and against which so much subsequent debate has been pitched, is a dualism of extended body and thinking mind. If thought is seen as the sole function of the mind, then animals – although clearly conscious – are seen as mindless.

FORM AND CHANGE

It is worth taking Aristotle's argument into account when considering the process of change and personal identity. When particular material parts of oneself change – whether through amputation or ageing – there remains an overall form that realizes the capacities of the body, and gives it coherence. That is the soul, or substance, or form; it is what is distinctive about each living thing. To change the form of something, it would be necessary to change the whole meaning and essence of the thing – form isn't located, but is a principle of definition and of recognition; it makes a thing what it is.

Suppose you fall into the hands of a skilled transplant surgeon. He (or she) can remove bits of your body and replace them by others. You gradually find yourself composed of bits of material that were not part of the original you. But you still have an identity, because your essence is the overall shape (not physical shape, but the sense of who you are) given to that material, and this cannot be considered on the same level as the bits and pieces that are removed and replaced. Form or essence is holistic; it is what the whole of you is, and does not depend upon the various parts of which you are composed.

In Mary Shelley's *Frankenstein*, there is a dramatic moment when the creature that Frankenstein has constructed from various human 'materials' comes to life. Soon this monstrous replica of a human being starts to develop thought and emotion, and responds with horror to the enormity of its artificial birth and the fact that it has been constructed in isolation, devoid of society and a normal personal history – with terrible results.

Frankenstein exposes the hubris of science, which assumes that it can analyse and then reassemble the human person without paying a terrible price for venturing into an area in which mechanical analysis and assembly simply will not suffice. Any human subject, viewed merely as a construction of parts, becomes a monster.

BODY AND SOUL

If the soul is what gives the body its form, bringing it forth as a living individual, then we need to recognize just how close the relationship between body and soul becomes. We do not have a body, with its own form and performing its own actions, to which a secondary, invisible thing called a 'soul' is added. The term 'soul' describes that which shapes and gives life to the body.

Consider the analogy of the actor on stage. The performer transforms himself or herself into the character being portrayed. That character is displayed in terms of words, actions, gestures and responses. The question to consider is how the actor relates to the character:

- ▶ The Aristotelian approach is to see the soul as the character being displayed, not as some hidden actor behind that character.
- ▶ The Platonic approach is to see the soul as more like the actor, with an eternal and therefore ongoing life quite apart from this particular character and performance.

Later Greek thought

Some later philosophers were to revert to more materialist ways of thinking about the self. Epicurus (341–271 BCE), like Democritus earlier, took an atomist view of reality. That is, he thought that the whole of reality could be seen as made up of physical bodies (atoms) in a void. The soul or self could not be void; therefore he needed to find some way of describing it in physical terms. He saw it as atoms, spread throughout the body, animating it – rather like a wind passing through and around a physical structure. The problem was always how this kind of physical reality could be related to the process of thought and perception.

Epicurus and others objected to the Platonic notion of an immortal and immaterial substance on the grounds (among others) that such a *psyche* could neither act nor be acted upon, since it would have no direct link with the physical and mutable world.

Insight

Notice here a fundamental feature of the mind/body problem. If the mind is physical, it is difficult to see how it can originate the sense of freedom and choice, since it is fixed within the web of physical causality. On the other hand, if it is not physical, it is difficult to see how it can exert an influence on the physical world. *In other words – putting it crudely – either it's not free to decide what to do, or it can't do it.*

The Stoics considered the soul to be like breath (*pneuma*), permeating and animating the body, giving it the ability to move about and relate to the world. They also introduced an important concept – that of representations (*phantasia*). When we perceive something, an idea of that thing is formed in the mind – a 'representation' of the object. We cannot know anything except by way of these representations. We must also have a perception of ourselves, before we can start to be aware of our world. Even animals, by showing fear in the face of something stronger then themselves, or aggression in the face of an attacker, must have some awareness of what they are, and of their relative place in the scheme of things. Without such basic awareness, their responses to the external world would make no sense.

The Stoics went one step further, and claimed that whatever was known through representations could also be described. Every representation has its *lekton*, or ability, to be articulated. In other words, the mind plays an important role in receiving and naming experiences. But such reception is only half the story. The mind then gives assent to what it perceives. In other words, it makes value judgements, either approving or disapproving of something and then acting accordingly.

According to Epictetus (55–135 CE), our personal identity comes from our moral character, which consists in making good use of the representations (*phantasia*) we receive. The self is not simply our reasoning faculty, but the application of our reason in selecting our goals and shaping our course in life. For a Stoic, this highlights a fundamental difference between a human being and an animal. Animals simply respond automatically to the stimuli they are given. A human being is able to reflect on the stimuli, to appreciate them and to choose how to respond to them. The whole of moral and social life follows from this.

Insight

The interest here has shifted from physical considerations of how a non-extended thing such as a soul can encounter the world, to seeing what it *does* about it. We may not be able to show exactly how our experience matches reality, but we at least know that we do have experiences and *we display our selfhood by the way in which we deal with them.*

The Stoics saw the whole of the self's controlling power (its *hegemonikon*), located in the heart, as responsible for the process of receiving and responding to impressions from outside. They did not separate out the rational aspects, nor did they speak of a self that was separable from the physical body through which it acted.

Against the Stoics, Plotinus (205–270 CE) and other Neoplatonists continued the tradition of the separate soul and body, although they generally held that the brain was the seat of the perceptions. They considered the self to be both aware and self-aware at the same time, and that the whole of the self was present in every part of the body. In other words, unlike the Stoics, they were concerned to remove any possibility of physical location; the soul was real, but not physical.

Plotinus discusses the soul in Book 4 of his *Enneads*. The soul was distinct from the body, because the body itself was composite and needed to be ordered, directed and given life by the soul. Without the soul, the body is dissolved. Notice here that there is a restatement of the Platonic dualism of soul and body, but taking into account some elements of Aristotle's view of the soul as giving form and order. This reflects the general position of the 'Neoplatonists', who would not have thought of themselves as having that label, but were simply restating Plato in the light of subsequent criticism.

As with the later medieval thinkers, there is also an important religious and moral element here. This physical life is essentially evil and limited, whereas the soul can look forward to its own good through the exercise of virtue and anticipate a non-physical destiny. The soul is superior to the body, although (at least in this life) it is expressed *through* the body, which it fills and directs.

Plotinus also saw the soul as descending into matter, passing through the various heavenly realms as it did so, and therefore he was able to argue that the patterns of the heavenly bodies could influence our earthly life, since at one time, before our appearance on earth, we had a celestial body. Thus, the soul arrives on earth with its character and dispositions already formed, and after this life it is destined to ascend again to the higher realm.

A review of the options

- ▶ For the Neoplatonists, as for Plato, the soul was essentially immortal and separable from the body.
- ▶ For the Epicurean, it was a fine physical substance.
- ▶ For Aristotle, it was the form of the body.
- ▶ For the Stoics, the soul was that which was self-aware, and also which encountered and understood the world through 'representations' and therefore language, issuing in the ability to evaluate and act morally. To use the modern term, the Stoics saw the self in terms of 'consciousness'.

It is commonly pointed out that most issues in Western philosophy can be traced back to ancient Greece, and the philosophy of mind is no exception. The Atomists and Epicureans took a view that has echoes in modern materialism and behaviourism, since they saw the mental aspects of life as embodied. By contrast, the Platonic approach, separating mind and body, leads to modern dualism. The Aristotelian and Stoic views have mind and body as distinct, but much more closely linked, with the Stoics anticipating much modern thought in terms of distinctive human self-expression and language.

As we shall see in the next chapter, many of the issues from the time of Descartes into the 20th century, arose from the desire to make a clear distinction between mind and body, and yet recognize the degree to which mind interacts with the physical world. The arguments may have changed, but the issues were very familiar to the ancient Greeks.

The soul and its fate

In assessing medieval views of the soul or self, it is important to recognize that, prior to the 13th century when Aristotle's works were translated and studied in European universities, there was a lack of secular philosophy, in the sense of a discussion of key issues without reference to an overall religious view of life, and even then, thinkers like Aquinas saw it as their task to reconcile such philosophy with Christian teaching. Hence the title of this section – 'The soul and its fate' – aims to reflect the concerns of religious thinkers during that period.

Of ancient philosophy, the tradition that most directly influenced the development of Christian thought was that of Plato, although there were also influences from the Stoics. This is seen particularly in writings of St Augustine (354–430), who contrasted the changing and fallen nature of the physical world, with the unchanging, eternal real of ideas. He saw the soul as a special substance whose task was to rule the body. It was endowed by God with reason, and could only be known through reason. Of course, he also believed that through the 'Fall' humankind was not as God had intended it to be, and that its intellect was dimmed and its will weakened. Hence, unaided human reason was unlikely to comprehend the mysteries of God or the self.

Nevertheless, in contrast to the material body, the mind was able to rise above the changing world and have true knowledge of immutable ideas. Augustine thought that the mind could be known through introspection and – anticipating Descartes' famous conclusion 'I think, therefore I am' – argued (in Book 10 of *De Trinitate*) that the existence of the mind was certain, for even if (following the sceptics) he could believe that he was deceived about most things, nevertheless, in order to be deceived, he must exist (*si fallor sum*) and could therefore never be deceived about his own existence.

Insight

Augustine also took the view that the senses themselves could not provide us with true knowledge but only the sensations that are the basis of knowledge. True knowledge required the exercise of reason to interpret those sensations. Augustine here anticipates modern discussions (see Chapter 6).

Thus, for Augustine, the mind is a divine gift, ruling the body, linking with the eternal world of ideas, and knowable only by reflection. This provides a very clear dualism of body and mind, which was to influence Descartes and, through him, much of the modern debate about the philosophy of mind.

The self or soul was thus seen as fallen, inhabiting a physical body but essentially connected with the higher world. At death, body and soul separate, the body to return to corruption, the soul to go to judgement and either heaven or hell. For religious reasons, therefore, it was crucial that body and soul were separable. Any theory which made the soul a by-product of bodily processes (the 'epiphenomenon' of later debates) would fail to take into account either its being a divine endowment, or its being able to have an eternal destiny once its temporal body was no more.

What is clear is that religion shaped both the questions asked and the conclusions reached, but that in itself does not count either for or against the truth of those conclusions. Indeed, the recognition that our ideas of self are bound up with issues of free will, morality and sense of personal destiny could equally apply to a secular existentialist viewpoint as a religious one.

Insight

It was inevitable that the thinking of Augustine and Aquinas would be shaped by their religion, but it may equally be true that some recent materialist arguments are the product of a determination to avoid anything that might smack of religion. For philosophy, the important thing is to weigh the arguments and explore their implication with an open mind; otherwise, the attempt either to promote or avoid religion may distort our thinking.

10 THINGS TO KEEP IN MIND

1 The Greeks distinguished between *psyche* and *nous*.

2 Plato has a dualist view of the body and soul.

3 Plato recognizes three elements in the self: mind, executive functions and appetite.

4 For Plato (and later Christian thought), the self aims to transcend the physical body.

5 Aristotle sees the *psyche* as the principle of life, distinguishing living things from inanimate objects.

6 For Aristotle, the soul is what gives something its particular essence.

7 Epicurus (like Democritus earlier) described the self in physical terms, as atoms spread through and animating the body.

8 The Stoics discussed mental representations (*phantasia*) of experiences, with which the self has to deal.

9 Augustine could not be deceived about his own existence.

10 Most debates in the medieval period were influenced by a religious agenda.

2

Descartes' legacy

In this chapter you will:
- *consider the contribution of Descartes*
- *explore various forms of dualism and idealism*
- *examine whether mind can emerge from matter.*

The philosophy of mind explores a whole range of possible relationships between mind and body, and some thinkers want to eliminate either one or the other. On the one side there is the idea that all that exists is the physical world, examinable by science (*materialism* and *behaviourism*); on the other is the less common view that all we can know are the phenomena we experience in our minds, and that it is the physical world that is uncertain, or only known through or put together by the mind (*idealism*).

Other philosophers take the view that both minds and bodies are real and related to one another (*dualism*). How exactly they are related is a further problem, and so we have a whole variety of forms of dualism, reflecting different ideas about that relationship.

Dualism

Although we have already come across dualism in Plato and in Augustine, in terms of the modern debate about minds and bodies, the most significant thinker was René Descartes (1596–1650). Many of the theories about how minds and bodies affect one another have developed in order to answer questions raised by Descartes' theory.

'I THINK THEREFORE I AM'

At a time when scepticism was rife, Descartes was concerned to find some point of certainty, from which he could start to build up a structure of genuine knowledge. He was aware that his senses could sometimes deceive him, and therefore resolved never to trust them. He supposed that some malign force was able to make him doubt all that he generally accepted as true. Was there anything that he could not doubt?

His conclusion – one of the most famous in the history of philosophy – was that he could not doubt himself as a thinking being, for the very act of doubting required thought: *cogito ergo sum*, 'I think, therefore I am.'

But what was this self that Descartes could not doubt? His conclusion implied a radical distinction between the world of matter, known to the senses, and the mental world, known (at least in one's own case) directly. Whereas he could doubt the existence of his body, he could never doubt that he had a mind, and therefore concluded that the mind must be clearly distinct from the body and that mind and matter were utterly different things. Matter was extended in space; mind was unextended. Matter was known to the senses; mind was not.

This radical dualism immediately caused problems. First of all, the 'self' was now reduced to just one aspect of being a person – thought. Humans were mechanical bodies, with unextended minds attached. How then could you ever know anybody else's mind? You could not encounter it through the senses, for it was not part of the physical world. How might your own mind actually make a difference in the physical world?

Insight

Descartes was writing at a time when the newly established sciences thought of the world in mechanical terms. Hence his concern to show how a thinking being might be able to effect a physical change; he wanted a view of the self that was compatible both with his religious instinct about the self and God and with his recognition of the claim of the sciences to explain everything in terms of causes.

Before examining dualism any further, one needs to guard against seeing the mind as some kind of subtle, invisible body, existing in the world of space and time, yet not subject to its usual rules of cause and effect. This is a rather crude caricature of what Descartes and other dualists have actually claimed, but it is a caricature that has often been taken for reality. It was presented by Gilbert Ryle in *The Concept of Mind* (1949), where he called Cartesian dualism the 'official view' and described it as 'the ghost in the machine'. He pointed out that Descartes tried to define the mind negatively, as that which was non-physical, non-extended and so on. As a result of this, he suggests that Descartes saw the mind as in some way as analogous to a body, but without the physical nature – in other words, as a non-physical machine. We shall look at this particular criticism a little later in this chapter.

The essential thing to recognize is that, for Descartes, mental reality is not a part of the physical world and therefore does not occupy space. The mind is not to be found in the brain, or any other part of the body. It may be related to the body, but is certainly not some occult set of physical causes and effects. That is why the 'ghost in the machine' is no more than a caricature.

Descartes considered that 'mind' was an immaterial substance, distinct from the physical substance of the body. Mental states were therefore related to this invisible thing. This is generally described as 'substance dualism' and has long since gone out of fashion, even among dualists.

MY MIND?

A key worry about Descartes' form of dualism is that one can refer to 'my mind'. But if 'my mind' means anything at all, then it implies that there is a sense of self that *transcends* the mind. If I were nothing but thought, then the conclusion to Descartes famous process of systematic doubt should not have been 'I think therefore I am' but simply 'There is thought'. The mere fact that thought is the one thing that cannot be doubted should not be taken to imply that a human being is *no more than* a thinking thing attached to a mechanical body. Few would challenge the idea that the process of thinking is a major part of what it is to be human; but is it all we mean by the self? Clearly, if 'my mind' has any significance, then it is not.

The real problem with Descartes' legacy on this issue is that generations of philosophers have struggled with the idea of mechanical bodies somehow taking on purposeful action, and wondering how on earth a non-physical, non-extended mind could bring that about.

However, it is difficult not to accept that the self is something different from the physical body. After all, most of the cells that go to make up your body will die off and be replaced over time. As an old person, you will not be recognizable as the baby you once were. Are you therefore different people as you go through life? Are you only identified by your memories (since that is the most obvious route to identifying yourself as an adult with your earlier experiences)? And if you lost your memory, would you therefore lose your self? We shall explore some of these issues in Chapter 7.

Interactionism

Dualism claims that mind and the body are distinct, but act upon one another. If you break a leg (a bodily phenomenon), you will experience pain (a mental phenomenon). If you get excited or afraid (or both at once!), your body reacts accordingly.

'Interactionism' is a general term for theories that seek to relate the distinct mental and physical realms to one another. There are many varieties of interactionism, some of which we shall outline here. All dualist theories need some form of interactionist argument to support them.

THE PINEAL GLAND

The problem Descartes faced was that he had a mechanical view of the physical world – and indeed, his mechanics depended upon the contact between bodies, without any of the benefit of Newton's idea of 'forces'. He therefore needed to show that there was some physical point in the body through which the non-physical, non-extended mind could actually operate to effect changes in the physical world.

In other words, he accepted that an absolute separation of mind and body could not be possible, for otherwise the mind could make absolutely no difference. Without some point of interaction there was no way of explaining how mental actions (e.g. feeling something or wanting something) can have physical results (e.g. flinching in response to pain or reaching out to take the desired object).

Descartes believed that the point of contact was the pineal gland, located between the left and right sides of the brain. He considered – thinking in terms of contact mechanics – that the very slightest movement in this gland would generate movement in the 'animal spirits' which, flowing through the body, would cause movement.

> **Insight**
>
> How an unextended mind could cause even the slightest movement in a physical body remained a theoretical problem – but Descartes tucked that problem away in the most inaccessible place possible. In doing so, he dodged the fundamental issue that his dualism had raised.

OCCASIONALISM

Occasionalism – a theory associated particularly with Nicolas Malebranche (1638–1715) – takes Descartes' dualism to its logical conclusion. If mind and body are completely separate, there seems no way that the one can have a direct causal effect on the other; there is no mechanism for getting across what was to become known as 'Leibniz's gap'. How then could mental events and physical events fit so closely together that they give the impression of being causally linked? How is it that, at the moment I feel pleased to see someone, my mouth stretches out in a smile?

Malebranche's answer to this is that, at the same moment that I feel happy, my face smiles. The two things happen separately but on the same occasion, and they are kept synchronized by God. I feel happy; God stretches my mouth.

> **Insight**
>
> This has always seemed to me to be a most implausible theory, quite apart from any issues of religious belief. If there is no mechanism that will allow my mind to influence the physical world, how does God do so? Presumably, God is not thought of as a physical being – so what enables his 'mind' to establish a mechanism to do what mine cannot?

PRE-ESTABLISHED HARMONY

Still on the religious theme, we come to Gottfried Wilhelm Leibniz (1646–1716), whose concept of pre-established harmony goes beyond Malebranche, in that God does not have to intervene constantly to ensure that my body does what my mind would like to do but cannot. Leibniz argued that there is a harmony between mind and matter that has been established by God, such that, although the mind appears to be directing what happens to the physical body, in actual fact the physical body is running within an enclosed physical system that only happens to coincide with the mental one. Between the two there remains the 'gap' (hence the term 'Leibniz's gap' for the disjunction of mind and body).

The mind does not actually make any difference to the physical world, in the sense of being a cause of physical movement, but only appears to do so, because of the coincidence of the two systems.

This theory is closely linked to Leibniz's view of physical reality. He held that everything is divisible again and again until you arrive at the simplest possible entities. But these could not have physical extension (for, if they did, they could be divided further), and if they are not physical, they must be mental, since (following Descartes) everything is either physical and extended, or mental and unextended. Leibniz called these entities *monads*. Every complex being therefore comprises countless monads. How do they all work together to produce intelligent activity? Leibniz argued that there must be a pre-established harmony, without which their organization would be quite impossible.

Clearly, Leibniz had a good religious reason for taking this view. It enabled him to introduce the idea of purpose back into a universe that could otherwise be seen as an impersonal mechanism. He saw purpose and cooperation between mechanical entities as established by God. It is only natural, therefore, that the harmony between mental volition and physical action should follow from this same fundamental, purposive ordering of nature.

....

Insight

Utterly unfashionable today and entirely innocent of psychology and neuroscience, to say nothing of religious criticisms of their deist view of God, these arguments highlight a fundamental problem that remains with us. The physical world, as described by science, is void of meaning, purpose, minds and God. It is a closed system of material causes. Even if we dismiss the simplistic religious answers proposed here, we are left with the inescapable fact that we, as human beings, have minds, live purposefully and engage with the world using a framework of meaning. Our *experience* of the world presupposes that the mental and the physical are intimately related to one another, as every purposeful act we carry out illustrates. Experience thus denies the very 'gap' that logic and science demand.

EPIPHENOMENALISM

From an evolutionary perspective, it is clear that the more advanced and complex a creature, the more likely it is for it to have what we would recognize as a mind or consciousness. Comparing something as complex as the brain and nervous system of a human being with that of some primitive creature, or with an inanimate object, it seems clear that the mind is in some way a product of the complexity of physical systems.

This approach leads to the view that mind is the natural *by-product* of an increasingly complex brain and nervous system. The various things that I think about, imagine or picture in my mind are therefore *epiphenomena*. They arise out of (and are caused by) neural activity, but they are not actually *part of* those physical phenomena – they are 'above' (*epi-*) them.

Now there is one obvious but crucial problem with this approach, namely that the mind becomes impotent. If it is produced by the physical system, rather than being able to interact with it, it cannot make a difference. Consciousness does not modify behaviour, for behaviour is part of the physical world, influenced only by physical causes – at most, conscious may give us the *illusion* of control. The smell of cooking may tell you what is going on in the oven, but the smell does not influence the process of cooking. So, if mental phenomena are given off by brain activity, they may show you what is happening, but cannot themselves make anything happen.

This theory allows the physical world to retain its closed system of causality. The fact that the mind is produced by the brain explains why physical and mental operations fit together, giving us the impression that our mind controls our body. Thus, for example, my arm needs to be raised and my brain puts this into effect, but at the same time there is the additional effect of a 'mental' product, namely my desire to raise my arm and the sense that I am causing it to rise. But the crucial thing here is that the mental product has not pre-dated the process that will lead to the arm being raised.

Insight

This has always struck me as one of the daftest of the many daft theories in the philosophy of mind. It goes counter to experience, where the decision to act, or even the process of worrying about whether or not to act, comes before the action itself. Watching a cat about to pounce on a mouse, or a child waiting for exactly the moment to press a button in a computer game, there is a complex set of relationships between observational inputs and the anticipation of a physical output. The process of holding one's breath and waiting for exactly the right moment is one that requires mental effort, and is a sign of the sophistication of sentient beings. To see that mental activity simply as by-product of a set of physical causes seems highly improbable. It makes sense only if we are thinking of 'mind' in the crudest form of substance dualism. The complexity of the operation that, on a physical level, the brain carries out is what we describe as and experience as the working of a conscious mind.

It is difficult to see how an epiphenomenalist position could really explain the process of writing a novel, for example. If the mind is simply a by-product of physical brain activity, with no way of influencing physical action, then the novel is not something 'thought up' at all. It is not the product of creative thought, but the inevitable result of a set of physical causes operating *in the present*. How then do you account for the premeditated sequence of words, paragraphs and chapters? Physical causality operates in the present; it does not anticipate the future nor does it remember the past – yet the act of writing, and thinking about what to write, requires tensed time.

Insight

How, on this theory, could anyone distinguish between a creative activity and a purely mechanical one? How do I know you are an intelligent individual rather than a robot, if whatever mind you have cannot have any effect on your speech or actions? In the end, epiphenomenalism seems little more than materialism with a private picture show attached!

'DOUBLE-ASPECT' THEORY

Baruch Spinoza (1632–77) took the view that God and nature were one and the same, and that all reality had both a mental and a physical aspect to it. Rather than having two very different substances, physical and mental, Spinoza argued that there was a single substance that was both conscious and extended. The mind and body could not be separated, and were in effect two ways of seeing the same thing. Everything we experience as mental must therefore also have a physical aspect.

This view, sometimes called the 'identity hypothesis', effectively argues that neural events and conscious experiences are simply two ways of explaining the same thing. In other words, thinking is the inner aspect of which the outer, or scientifically examinable, aspect is brain activity.

In terms of a description of what is going on when an intelligent action is being performed, one could say that human beings have mental properties that are non-physical, but that such properties do not imply that there is a separate, non-physical 'substance' called mind.

Property dualism

The dualism of Descartes, as we have seen is one that distinguished between two forms of *substance*: physical and mental. More recent forms of dualism tend to let go of the idea of substance, and focus on *properties*. In other words, there are different levels at which a complex entity can be considered and described. Mental properties are applied to a level of complexity – i.e. the workings of a complex being as a whole, as opposed to the workings of the individual parts that make it up – that is quite different from that to which physical properties apply. For *property dualism* the same complex physical thing has two very different sets of properties, with mental properties not reducible to physical ones.

One of the problems with this idea – both in Spinoza's approach, and in modern property dualism – is that, if mental attributes are applied to the same reality as physical attributes, then it would seem that causality, which appears to determine all that happens in the physical world, will therefore remove all freedom from intelligent human action. Freedom becomes an illusion.

But perhaps there is a more general point that needs to be made about dualism. If we see it as the attempt to look at two separate 'things', mind and matter, we will always struggle to see how they can mesh together, and there will always be a temptation to simplify matters by reducing one to the other. It may be more useful to think in terms of the difference between the objective or scientific examination of life, and *the experience of life as it is lived*. This may appear as a form of the 'double-aspect' approach, but it is not so much two ways of looking at the mind and the body, but two ways in which mind and body together experience the world.

The 'ghost in the machine'

The Concept of Mind (1949) by Gilbert Ryle was an enormously influential book. It applied a linguistic approach to philosophy (which was of growing significance for philosophy at that time) to the issues of mind. In other words, it was concerned with concepts and their meaning – asking questions like 'What does it mean to call an action intelligent?'

Ryle suggested that to speak of minds and bodies as though they were equivalent things was to make a 'category mistake'. So, to use one of his own examples:

> 'A foreigner watching his first game of cricket learns what are the functions of the bowlers, the batsmen, the fielders, the umpires and the scorers. He then says "But there is no one left on the field to contribute the famous element of team-spirit. I see who does the bowling, the batting and the wicket-keeping; but I do not see whose role it is to exercise *esprit de corps*."'

Clearly, the term *esprit de corps* is used to describe the way in which all this is done, but it is not identified with any one distinct function. Similarly, therefore, he argues that 'mind' does not describe something over and above the various physical actions that intelligent beings carry out; it simply describes them as intelligent. To make a 'mental' activity take place alongside various physical activities is to commit a category mistake:

> 'My destructive purpose is to show that a family of radical category-mistakes is the source of the double-life theory. The representation

of a person as a ghost mysteriously ensconced in a machine derives from this argument.'

Essentially, Ryle shifts the mind/body problem. Instead of asking how we know that physical behaviour is influenced by a non-physical mind, the task he sets himself is to define what sort of criteria can be used to decide if, for example, the adjective or adverb 'intelligent' has been correctly ascribed.

Ryle's target is what he called the 'official' view, stemming from Descartes, which he calls the doctrine of the 'ghost in the machine'. He says of it:

'It maintains that there exist both bodies and minds; that there occur physical processes and mental processes; that there are mechanical causes of corporeal movements and mental causes of corporeal movements. I shall argue that these and other analogous conjunctions are absurd; but, it must be noticed, the argument will not show that either of the illegitimately conjoined propositions is absurd in itself. I am not, for example, denying that there occur mental processes. Doing long division is a mental process and so is making a joke. But I am saying that the phrase "there occur mental processes" does not mean the same sort of thing as "there occur physical processes", and, therefore, that it makes no sense to conjoin or disjoin the two.'

Ryle therefore wants to say that mental descriptions (e.g. 'intelligent') are simply ways of describing particular kinds of physical activity. I cannot look inside a person's mind and see their intelligence; I can only infer it from what they say and do. *In other words, I can have 'mind talk', without having to accept the existence of a separate substance called 'mind'.*

A key feature of Ryle's view is that it is a mistake to say that *your mind* did something; rather you should simply say that *you* did it. In other words, Ryle argued that to say a person is kind is not describing a quality in some unobservable 'mind', but simply describing a feature of the attitudes and behaviour of that person. Mental predicates apply to a person, not to something called his or her 'mind'.

But it is one thing to say that mental predicates can be explained in terms of physical actions, quite another to say that those mental predicates can be *identified with, or reduced to*, the physical actions through which they are expressed.

Example

You see an actress express a whole range of emotions on stage; you see her angry or sad or elated. There need be no doubt in your mind what emotion is being shown, it is clear. Now we have no privileged access to the actress's mind. We simply see what she shows, and she shows those emotions by imaginatively entering into the drama that has been scripted for her. So far, so Ryle – no problem. But, we know that the emotions are not those of the actress herself, but only of the part she is playing.

Now if the actions and gestures were taken to be *identical* to the emotions, then the actress would indeed suffer bereavement, elation or whatever every time she went on stage. That cannot be the case. Deception and play-acting are only possible because we habitually use physical actions, words and gestures to indicate what a person thinks and feels. We may be deceived, and deception requires that there is something which is hidden from us – namely whether the external appearances do in fact depict what that person is thinking and feeling.

One of the problems with Ryle's approach is that, because it equates a mental state with a physical disposition, it is difficult to take into account the influence of one mental state on another. And yet we are all the time open to many different (and sometimes conflicting) desires and beliefs, which influence how we behave.

For example, someone on hunger strike is offered food. He refuses it. If the mental experience of hunger is defined as the desire to eat food, then at that moment the hunger striker is not hungry. But that is crazy: he is hungry, but refuses food on principle. It is difficult to see how such internal debates, overriding expected activity, can be accounted for if all mental states are ultimately reduced to actions and dispositions to act. Ultimately, Ryle seems to make the mistake of identifying the *criteria* for ascribing mental predicates with the mental properties themselves.

Insight

One wonders just how worldly-wise some philosophers are. Have they never played games of bluff, or tried to fool opponents into thinking that they have a better set of cards in their hand than is actually the case? Have they never tried to appear stern, while suppressing hilarity, in reprimanding a child who has done something outlandishly naughty? Have they never deceived, even just a little, in the game of love?

In the real world, thoughts, feelings, hopes, desires and all the deviousness of a mind that seeks its own ends, comes first and actions follow. That is the way human beings operate. They also become adept at watching for the gullible, interpreting body language, and generally trying to get ahead in the game of guessing what others are thinking and feeling.

INTERPRETING ACTION

Ryle suggests that we can apply mental predicates to physical actions – that is, that an action is 'clever'. Mental descriptions are generally statements about dispositions to act in a particular way. The problem is that, when we come to describe action, we are actually interpreting, rather than describing, what we see. The ascriptions 'clever' or 'cunning', for example, do not refer to the particular action, but to an interpretation of the significance of that action in its context. The action becomes cunning because it is clearly part of a strategy, aimed at some future goal.

But here we hit a problem, for the interpretation presupposes exactly what Ryle wants to avoid. 'Cunning' does describe the action, but not simply its physical attributes. Another person might do exactly the same thing, but might not be described as cunning. Cunning presupposes that forethought, planning, means and ends – in other words, mental operations, the very things that Ryle says we cannot treat as causes of physical actions – are there in the description of that action.

It is a key feature of experience that we always experience things 'as' something, and that 'as' is an interpretation and thus a feature contributed by our mind. Our senses may register a blob of red with a distinctive scent; our mind registers 'rose'. All descriptions of physical behaviour, far from being 'all there is' when it comes to describing another person, require the idea of mind to make sense of them.

A 'PLACE' FOR MIND?

It is clear that Ryle will not accept anything that sets mental and physical attributes alongside one another as though they belonged to the same category, and accuses traditional dualism of doing just that. But there are two important points to make about his criticism:

1 It is possible to be a dualist without holding, as Descartes did, that the mind is completely separate and distinct from the body, with the one physical and extended and the other not. It is possible to have a dualism of properties, rather than of substances. In other words, one could see a human being as a physical structure, but one that has two sets of properties. One set comprises physical data, colour of hair, colour of eyes, height, weight and so one. The other comprises mental qualities: kind, selfish, thoughtful, irritable, experiencing pain or unhappiness. These refer to the same entity, but they are non-physical qualities that describe how that living organism relates to its stimuli, and – in a sense – how it feels. Such non-physical qualities may be known through observation (I see someone running down the street with a broad grin on his or her face) or through the sharing of language (someone complains of pain, and I know what that word means, and can imaginatively enter into his or her situation because I have experienced things of the same sort myself). Hence I am not learning about some 'other' person, separate from the physical entity I see before me. Rather I see that person in a particular way, in terms of his or her response and communication – that is what yields the non-physical characteristics.

2 Descartes was not quite as simplistic as Ryle makes out. In saying that the mind is unextended, he implies that the mind does not exist in the same sense that physical things exist. The point at

which Descartes is vulnerable to Ryle's criticism, however, is his unfortunate idea about the pineal gland being the locus of mental causality within the physical realm. But once that is taken into account, the thrust of Ryle's criticism of dualism is effectively the same one that has been raised all along – namely that, given the physical world offers a seamless network of causes, it is simply not possible to specify in what way mind makes a difference, since all difference-making is automatically assumed to be accounted for by physical causes, whether known or unknown.

Supervenience

Life makes no sense without both the physical and the mental; that much is clear. For the traditional dualist, the problem is seeing how minds and bodies can influence one another – and yet all our experience confirms that they do.

Two ways out of this dilemma have yet to be described: idealism and materialism; the one reducing everything to mind, the other to matter. We have also seen that it is possible to see the mental and the physical as two ways of describing the same thing, or to regard the mental as no more than a by-product of the physical. But is there any other way in which mind and body can relate to one another?

When we analyse things, we generally reduce them to their component parts and examine how those parts relate to one another. For a materialist, a mental operation may thus be identified with the electrical and chemical changes in groups of neurons. Reality is assumed to be found at the finest level of detail.

However, it is possible to look at this from a very different perspective. As simple things gather together to form more complex units, so those units appear to have qualities that were not there in the simpler parts. Thus chemicals take on qualities that are not seen in atoms, and cells take on qualities not seen in their constituent chemicals. The further up the chain of complexity you go, the more qualities emerge that were not seen lower down.

So, in terms of biology, once you get to have individual living cells, they have the ability to take in nourishment and to reproduce. Life thus emerges from its constituent parts. Being a 'living thing' means

something – to be able to reproduce, for example that is real,
but which cannot be true of the simpler chemicals of which its cells
are composed.

Taking that a stage further, a human being has what we call
consciousness. We can think, choose, respond creatively to situations,
experience emotions, and decide how to act. But the various cells
that make up our bodies do not have those qualities or abilities:
consciousness emerges once life gets to a certain level of complexity.

Hence we have two terms that are used in modern discussion to cover
that situation: *emergence* and *supervenience*.

Emergence is the process just described. Supervenience describes
the way mental properties *supervene* on physical ones. The mental
description does not have to refer to something else. It is about the
same physical phenomenon as the ordinary physical description,
but it describes the situation from a 'higher' or more complex
perspective.

Notice that what we have here is another form of *property dualism*.
In other words, there are new properties that emerge in the complex
being that are not found in its more simple components. Mental
properties are very different from physical ones, and cannot be
reduced to them, but that does not have to imply that there is some
other non-physical world to which they belong.

Taking this view one could argue that mental properties *depend on*
physical ones, and hence it is compatible with a general physicalist
view. But at the same time mental properties remain distinct from the
physical and cannot be reduced to them.

Insight

The real problem with this approach is to know why it is that activity at one
level gives rise to activity at another. Why is it that 'pleasure' supervenes on
one set of physical stimuli and 'pain' on another? Just what mechanism is that
that can connect these different layers?

Although the idea of emergence may sound modern, linked perhaps
to evolutionary psychology, it is found in the work of John Locke
(1632–1710) who argued – in his third letter to Bishop Shillingford
of Worcester – that the vegetable part of nature is wholly material,
but has excellences not found in inanimate things, and that the

animal world similarly gains perfections and properties not found in matter in general. Of course, as is to be expected from that era, Locke regards the qualities of thinking and self-motion as being bestowed by an omnipotent power on certain parts of matter. And if it is objected that one cannot conceive how God might give a physical body the power to think, he would reply that there are many physical laws (e.g. gravity) that we cannot understand but we have to accept them anyway. Hence, not understanding how sense and voluntary motion can emerge from matter is no good reason to deny their existence.

PANPSYCHISM?

If mind emerges from matter, as a new set of properties, once a certain level of complexity has been reached, it raises the problem of exactly *when* that might happen. Let us assume for a moment that we are dealing with the broad Greek concept of *psyche*, rather than the narrower, Cartesian idea of the mind as exclusively the agent of thought. In terms of complexity, one can construct a hierarchy with humankind at the top (and with 100 billion neurons networked in the brain, we are the most complex thing yet encountered in the universe), and the most primitive form of life at the bottom. At what point on that hierarchy do you introduce *psyche*? Where, in the process of evolution, does it appear?

Biology specifies what counts as a living organism, in terms of its ability to take in food, to replicate itself and so on. Should we not therefore try to specify the minimum requirements for something to have a conscious *psyche*. Clearly, the more complex something is, the greater our ability to appreciate that it is conscious and relate to it in ways that assume its mental powers. You can train a dog, but not an earthworm. But if you touch an earthworm it responds. Should you not therefore ascribe to it some basic form of *psyche*? And what of microbes? A virus may be described as malignant, but that does not imply that it has malign intentions, simply that it reproduces itself in ways that threaten the wellbeing of its host. So perhaps a virus is off the scale, but where then does mind start?

Or – looking the other way – when does it *stop*? If you accept that *Homo sapiens* has a mind, what of the Neanderthals or the other hominids? At what point could you say that the brain capacity is insufficient to justify the ascription of mental life? Are higher apes, then, mindless?

So, if mind emerges from matter in some automatic way related to complexity, we have at least the logical possibility that mind exists everywhere in some primitive form – that everything has some sort of interior life (a view termed 'panpsychism'). The question then becomes at what point does reflective thought appear over and above basic consciousness. If we follow Descartes and think of the mind mainly in terms of rational thought, then all other animals are mindless automata; if we accept the *psyche* as a broad description of sentience and response to the environment, it is found at some level in a wide variety of life forms.

Insight

This approach is often neglected in modern debate. Those wanting to follow up on it may explore Leibniz idea of 'monads', Spinoza's 'double-aspect' approach to reality, A.N. Whitehead's 'process philosophy', or even the 'complexity-consciousness' argument of the mid-20th-century Jesuit philosopher and scientist Teilhard de Chardin.

Idealism

We cannot know the world except in so far as it is mediated through experience, and thus through mind. Although we assume that there is a world 'out there', when we try to justify that assumption we are forced to recognize that it makes no sense to say that something exists independent of my (or someone's) experience of it, because there is no way to know anything exists except as an experience in a mind. The best-known exponent of this position is Bishop George Berkeley (1685–1753).

Physical objects, on Berkeley's reckoning, are no different from the sense impression that we have of them. In other words, we do not have a problem of asking how our image of the world compares with the world itself, because it is the world itself, as far as we are concerned. He argues (in *The Principles of Human Knowledge*) that the various sensations which, combined, are the way we understand the world, are dependent upon the perceiving mind.

To use Berkeley's own example, I can say that the table on which I write exists, because I can see and feel it. If out of the room, I can still say that the table exists, meaning that, if I or anyone else were to enter the room he or she would perceive it. It therefore makes no sense to say that it exists, except in the context of being perceived.

'To be is to be perceived' is the key to his approach; to be perceived with the qualities that our senses give something is what it means to say that something exists. What is fascinating about Berkeley's argument is how close it comes to the position of a very different group of philosophers – the 20th-century Logical Positivists. They, too, held that meaningful language had to be backed up by sense experience. What Berkeley accepted, but they did not, was that things continued to exist between being perceived by individuals, because they were constantly being perceived by God.

Berkeley's views are sometimes portrayed as quite unreasonable, and as going against common sense. In fact, his argument – that we can have no knowledge of the external world that is independent of our sensations (and thus of our mental activity) – has considerable force.

An experiment

To experience the strength of this argument, just look around you for a moment, keeping your head quite still. Be aware of colours, shapes, perhaps the touch of things close to you. See all these things as 'out there', beyond that great window between your ears through which you experience your vision of the world. Then close one eye, and gently press on one side of your other eyeball. Everything you see shifts a little. Hold that for a moment. Can you tell that is shifted? Reach out and touch something. Your experience of touch exactly matches your 'shifted' vision, as though giving confirmation that the shifted vision is in fact correct. Remove the pressure on the eyeball; the world shifts back to 'normal', and your touch confirmed that view as well. If it illustrates nothing else, this shows the extent to which the mind organizes the sensations it receives and compensates for any mismatch in the information received. If it did not, then your sense of touch would not have been experienced as exactly corresponding to your 'shifted' vision.

That may not lead you to say that the external world does not exist, but it is a reminder that the very solid 'external' world is, in reality, a mental construct, formed as your brain synthesizes the sense impressions it receives.

It is one thing to say that our knowledge of the world is mediated through the mind, quite another to say that everything is mind. However, let us press this a bit further. We know that matter is comprised of atoms, and within them subatomic particles. If the reality of the world is found in its constituent parts, then the reality of the world is not detectable by the unaided human senses. The world we know and within which we operate is one that is determined by our mind and sensory organs – they enable us to have a world.

Insight

The other inescapable fact is that – as the Buddha said – our life is the creation of our mind, in that it is our thoughts of yesterday that have shaped our present reality, and our thoughts of today will shape our future. In this way, within our given physical circumstances, our mind plays a crucial role in shaping who we are. If you doubt that, just reflect on the choices you have made in the past that have made you what you are today.

Idealism is fascinating as a theory of knowledge, but it has never been a popular option in terms of understanding the mind. Yet, if its attempt to reduce the physical world to the mind seems implausible, its logical problems are not so different from the more popular materialist attempt to reduce the mind to bits of material reality.

10 THINGS TO KEEP IN MIND

1 Descartes proposed a dualism of thinking mind and physical body.

2 The basic problem with dualism is to show how mind and body can interact.

3 Descartes thought that the point of interaction was the pineal gland.

4 Occasionalism and pre-established harmony take Cartesian dualism to its logical conclusion.

5 Epiphenomenalism sees mind as an impotent product of the brain and nervous system.

6 Spinoza's 'double-aspect' theory introduces 'property dualism'.

7 Ryle criticizes Descartes' theory as 'the ghost in the machine'.

8 Mental properties may emerge out of physical complexity.

9 Panpsychism sees everything as having *psyche* in some form.

10 Idealism sees all knowledge as dependent upon the mind.

3

Cognitive science

In this chapter you will:
- *explore the range of cognitive sciences*
- *examine the contribution of artificial intelligence*
- *consider the functionalist approach to mind.*

In turning to cognitive science, let us be clear about why this represents an entirely new approach to the philosophy of mind. We saw in the last chapter that Descartes' radical dualism of body and mind dominated the thinking in this area until the middle of the 20th century. Even those who dismissed talk of minds as being either meaningless or as covert ways of speaking about physical actions or appearances were nevertheless under the spell of the Cartesian view that the mind was, in some way, completely different from the physical body.

Dualist struggled to explain how the mental could influence the physical and vice versa, since there seemed to be no mechanism that could span the gulf between them. Behaviourists and materialists (whom we shall consider in Chapter 4) simply regarded the mental as a mistaken, even if convenient, way of speaking about collections of physical phenomena.

By the 1950s the problems in the philosophy of mind seemed straightforward, if insoluble. On the one hand there was the whole raft of questions associated with the inherent problems of dualism – knowledge of other minds, the possibility of disembodied existence and so on. On the other, there were debates about the status and verifiability (or otherwise) of language about minds and mental events, typified by Ryle's challenge to what he saw as the conventionally accepted view.

In a sense, the philosophical debates about mind became blocked at that level. Few doubted the phenomenon of mind – for, like Descartes, the act of doubting was itself seen as mental. Yet it was difficult to see how the dualistic gulf could be bridged and how the mental could be examined in empirical and scientific terms.

Into this situation there came new academic disciplines:

- ▶ **Linguistics** was a development of the philosophy of language, seeking to use a scientific approach to issues of communication.
- ▶ The rapid development of **computers** raised issues of whether it might be possible to construct a machine that could imitate the process of thought – or indeed, whether such a machine could be considered to be 'thinking'.
- ▶ **Neuroscience** and **pharmacology** were also examining the nature and working of the human brain and the effect of drugs on behaviour and 'mental' states.
- ▶ **Clinical psychology** had a contribution to make, since it considered the mind in terms of its function (both conscious and unconscious) in the life of the individual, rather than simply taking a behaviourist approach.

It was clear that the philosophy of mind could not long stand aloof from these allied disciplines, since they were covering very similar territory but from different (and largely scientific) starting points. Hence the term 'cognitive science', indicating an interdisciplinary and scientific area of study concerned both with the process of human cognition (the theory of knowledge that had previously been described as 'epistemology' in traditional philosophy) and issues connected to the brain and its relationship to thought, activity and communication. Its approach added scientific experiment and evidence to the traditional philosophical process of reflection, introspection and the analysis of language.

One thing to keep in mind here is that the early development of cognitive science followed the behaviourists in that it studied *observable phenomena*. The difference between cognitive science and behaviourism was the range of phenomena that were taken into consideration. As we shall see later in this chapter, the functionalist approach to the mind saw mental events and qualities as possibly expressed through a variety of different physical states (much as the a piece of computer software can run on different hardware)

– so it became theoretically possible to study mental phenomena without needing to have an exhaustive knowledge of the brain, or the workings of a computer memory chip. What mattered was the *function* of the mental quality, and this was largely independent of the physical environment in which it was operating. This tied in well with the development of artificial intelligence, since 'mental' phenomena were functions that could be performed in a simple way by computers as well as by human brains.

Insight

Whereas consciousness itself is what the mind *feels like* – in other words what it is like to be a thinking and feeling human being – cognitive science is the study of what the mind *does*. This distinction was set out clearly by David Chalmers in *The Conscious Mind* (1996)

Psychology

The functionalist approach to mind is also illustrated by the development of psychology as a science. The early 'structuralists' attempted to analyse all experience into its component sensations. So Wilhelm Wundt and others, working in the 1870s, hoped to discover the workings of the mind by asking subjects to reflect on their experience and report back on it. In this way they built up a detailed pattern for analysing experience. By doing this, however, they generally blurred a distinction between looking at what the mind does, and the reporting of the experiences of the mind. It was assumed that such detailed reporting was the only way to get information about the mind. In the end, this approach failed, since they had no means of knowing whether the reporting was accurate, since there was no way of checking sensations objectively.

In 1890 William James, who was for many years Professor of Psychology at Harvard, wrote *Principles of Psychology*, which became the standard textbook, and two years later *Psychology: The Briefer Course*. In these books, he looked at the function of the emotions and the way in which people can give physical expression to them. In particular, he suggested that emotions (or passions) could be cultivated by adopting the appropriate physical postures associated with them (to put it crudely: look good and you'll feel good; wave your fist in the air and courage will arise in you). He thought that the reverse was also true: that if you simply refused to give any physical expression to an emotion, it would die.

In terms of the philosophy of mind, this view has two significant implications:

1 That there is a constant two-way process of influence going on between minds and bodies; it is not simply that the mind controls the body.
2 That mental activity can be assessed by its method of expression – that is, the physical activity to which it gives rise. It became a relatively short step from that point to saying that shaking one's fist is what 'being angry' *really* means – the view later adopted by Ryle.

At the same time, Freud was developing his theory about the effect of the unconscious mind on the behaviour and attitudes of neurotic patients. In terms of the philosophy of mind, this illustrated that the mind (particularly the unconscious) could have a most profound effect on a person's wellbeing, without that person being able even to identify the root cause of his or her problems.

In a totally different direction, the behaviourist approach to psychology, seen particularly in the work of Ivan Pavlov (in Russia) and B.F. Skinner (in the USA), involved the testing of animals in controlled conditions, examining their responses to stimuli and their adopting of habitual patterns in order to make sense of their experience.

Insight

Notice that this approach had no need to posit internal, conscious mental states at all; all that was required was to measure stimulus and response. The 'internal' aspect was irrelevant to what was being examined. It provided scientific data but assumed that 'mind' was largely programmable and trainable – which has huge implications for human society; namely that, if you organize the right stimuli, people will act as planned.

A common feature of psychological approaches, however, was that they were considering the way the mind functions in the life of an individual. Whether it was the effect that trauma in early childhood, could have later in life, or the way in which a rat could learn to perform a simple operation in order to get more food, the functioning of the mind was being observed and recorded. It was not a matter of debating whether minds existed, but exploring how they did what they did. This was in line with increasingly 'functionalist' views of the mind that were emerging as a result of the study of artificial intelligence (see below).

Language and innate knowledge

Innate knowledge is an interesting touchstone for evaluating different theories of mind. There is a fundamental difference of approach between rationalists (e.g. Descartes) and empiricists (e.g. Hobbes or Locke). Those who take a rationalist approach may hold the view that some ideas are innate. In other words, that we are all born with a set of fundamental ideas and ways of thinking, and that it is only through these that we can understand the world as we do. This approach goes back to Plato, where we only know individual things because we have prior knowledge of the eternal 'Forms'. Indeed, Plato considered that true knowledge (as opposed to opinion) could not come through the senses, since they were always fallible.

Contrariwise, those who took the empiricist approach (that all knowledge comes through sense experience) were able to say that people have innate *capabilities*. In other words, that they are born with the ability to do certain things, including the ability to think and use language. What they cannot have, in the absence of empirical evidence provided by the senses, is innate *knowledge*.

Insight

Today we may claim that people are born already 'hard-wired' for certain things – in other words, that the brain is set up to allow them to happen. The issue, however, is whether what we are born with is *content*, or just *potential*. Without a sophisticated society, thought and language would not be possible; but, given the nature or our brains, were they inevitable?

CHOMSKY

Noam Chomsky (b. 1928) made a case for innate capabilities, in terms of the acquisition of language. He argued that children do not gradually learn the grammar of a language before they start to speak it. Rather, they seem to know how to put words together – that they have an innate sense of how language works. In other words, everyone is biologically programmed to speak a language.

In favour of this view was the fact that very different languages have deep structures that are very similar. Words and phrases may be different from anything that we have heard before, but we sense that we are listening to a language, not just a jumble of sounds. A child very quickly identifies that structure, and starts to communicate, even though its vocabulary may be very limited.

Competence in using a language is not the same thing as intelligence (as measured by IQ tests); it is something shared by all. A person may be highly articulate without being able to read or write. Learning a second language, of course, is a very different matter. We learn the grammar from books and struggle to get it right. Often the person who has a good working vocabulary in a foreign language, and who pronounces it well, may still lack the subtlety of phraseology and idiom that comes automatically to the untrained native speaker.

But is it possible to learn a new language if you do not already have a natural language? How could a new language make sense, unless you already have what amounts to an innate knowledge of the principles by which words are put together?

Contrast the way in which a second language is learned with that of the child who is developing his or her natural language. The rules of the new language are explained with reference to the natural one, and justified by the fact that the person already known that natural one. But how is that one justified? One would need to suggest some sort of pre-language, a body of innate rules for understanding what these strings of words signify. But how would you know that those rules are correct? Only by suggesting an even more basic one... and so on. This leads to an infinite regress. In order to justify *any* linguistic form, one needs to have some already accepted criterion by which to do so. The conclusion would seem to be that, *for any language to make sense, there must be some innate linguistic starting point, itself needing no further justification.*

WITTGENSTEIN

It is almost impossible to say anything about language without at some point mentioning Ludwig Wittgenstein (1889–1951). In his early work, *Tractatus Logico-Philosophicus*, he was concerned with the validation of language, particularly as it related to the criteria used by science – in other words, he wanted to show the logic and evidence that lay behind statements. In particular, his approach was one in which language had a 'picturing' function, with its truth or falsity depending on whether or not it corresponded to things and events in the world. In this, he places the self outside the world:

▶ The subject does not belong to the world, but is a limit of the world.
▶ This is most important, for any attempt to describe the self is going to fail if that language is required (in order to me meaningful) to 'correspond' to some physical state of affairs.

Insight

Whatever we describe, it cannot be the subject self, for as soon as we describe it, we externalize it and make it part of 'our' world, standing out there over against us. The self cannot describe itself, unless it tries to make itself an object. And if it tries to do that, it loses the very essence of its selfhood.

However, in his later philosophy Wittgenstein switched from seeing meaning in terms of 'picturing' to meaning in terms of *use*. If you want to understand a word, you have to see its context in which it is being used. Following this line of thought, one can therefore see the sense in understanding language about the mind and consciousness primarily in the context of what such language *does*. You describe feelings, for example, in order to communicate your hopes or wants to other people. You are not trying to give some alternative description of brain activity to a passing neuroscientist! The meaning of your thoughts and consciousness is therefore appreciated only within an appropriate context.

Key points

▶ The structure of language, whether it is innate or socially defined, reflects the structure of thought. As we think, we speak to ourselves, we puzzle out issues, hold inner dialogues, and weigh concepts. Language is a medium of communication simply because people share a common structure of thought – a structure which expresses itself through language, but is also shaped by language.

- ▶ Language is public. A private language makes no sense, since concepts are conventional and reflect communication. Otherwise, why should certain sounds take on meaning?
- ▶ If it were not for language, we would know only what we could experience for ourselves. Our past would be limited to our own memory, and our world would be limited to our visible horizon. In a real sense, although we would be conscious, and would be able to respond to stimuli, we would not be able to think in anything like the way we take for granted. We would look and see, but not be able to frame concepts to explain (to ourselves or others) *what* we see. Communal action would be based on signs and common intuition, and therefore limited to the most primitive of need satisfaction.
- ▶ The philosophy of mind is a study of that which is *expressed through* and largely *generated by* language. The mind involves consciousness, memory and language. But consciousness and memory without language are no more than visual images, feelings and instinctual responses. Reflective consciousness, which is a distinctively human trait, requires language.

Evolutionary psychology

Is it possible to find a point in the history of life on this planet when 'mind' or 'consciousness' emerged? Is it possible to look back at very simple organisms and trace the moment when they can be said to be sentient, in other words, to be aware of their environment and to respond to it?

Clearly, different species of animals have different minds, with different abilities and levels of thought. What are the features of the development of *Homo sapiens* that has led to our present mental abilities?

These questions, looking at the function of mind in different species, gives an interesting slant on the human mind, and particularly on its social nature. These things are explored by, for example, Daniel Dennett in his books *Darwin's Dangerous Idea* (1995) and *Kinds of Minds* (1996).

Different species behave in very different ways, and that it is dangerous to project onto one the thoughts of another. So, for example, ants work away within a community, carrying out their respective roles quite selflessly. But are they thinking about such things? Do they feel a responsibility to carry refuse away from the nest, for example? Or are they operating in mechanical and programmed ways, with none of the subtlety of the mental operations of more advanced species (advanced, that is, from a human perspective)? And how could we know whether an ant is thinking about what it is doing, or is simply getting on and doing it, mindlessly? If we knew why consciousness and mind has developed differently in different species, it might give us valuable insights into what mind actually is.

Evolution has become the scientific paradigm at the biological level. It is natural therefore to ask whether the theory of evolution might have something to contribute to our knowledge of the mind. Everything can be evaluated in terms of evolutionary advantage; and if that applies to physical characteristics, it should equally apply to the mind. So what is it about having a consciousness and thought that gives an evolutionary advantage?

Example

Let us consider therefore a simple mental ability that could give evolutionary advantage: the recognition of individual features.

▶ If it were impossible to recognize individuals, then everyone might be a friend or an enemy, a threat or a source of help. In a situation of some danger, it is therefore essential to be able to recognize those who belong to your own tribe or family, in order to be able to combine resources in the struggle for existence.
▶ Hence, the ability to recognize kinship is an important step towards banding together in kinship groups for mutual protection.
▶ The one who remains a 'loner' becomes vulnerable.
▶ The ability to co-operate with others will increase success in hunting and killing larger animals that might threaten a lone hunter.
▶ Hence the mental ability to see, recognize and remember the appearance of kin gives an evolutionary advantage – hence it is a mental ability that will increase over time.

Of course, the one thing that has given humankind the most important evolutionary advantage has been the development of language. With language, knowledge can be passed on from one generation to the next, and therefore accumulates quickly. Without language, everything has to be learned from scratch with each new generation, and that is a great limitation.

Evolution depends upon success in coping with the environment – those who gain an advantage by having a particular quality breed and therefore increase the number of members of their species with that quality in the future. The brain is a key feature in looking at the rise of the higher apes and up to *Homo sapiens*; there has been a significant increase in brain capacity as evolution towards humankind has progressed.

But the mechanism for developing the brain is the success that mental activity gives for survival in a competitive environment. Those who are able to devise tools to plan out strategies in co-operation with others are at an advantage. Larger brains make these functions possible. As we evolve as individuals, we go through a similar process of mental development. We are born with far more neural connections than we will ever use, and we gradually – as we encounter the world and discover what we can do in it – build up patterns of brain activity, corresponding to our growing consciousness of the world.

In other words, the brain is the physical organ through which we lay down our experiences as memories, and are thus able to learn, communicate, think and organize our lives. That gives us an evolutionary advantage, and explains why the brain has increased in volume over time.

Dennett sees the mind as made up of many devices that have a long evolutionary history. From the crude intentionality of simple creatures, to the mind of human beings, there is a development – through the process of natural selection – in the direction of increased awareness of, and sophisticated response to, the environment.

However, it is not always obvious that consciousness gives an evolutionary advantage. As Ray Tallis has pointed out (see Further reading), unconscious mechanisms generally act faster than conscious ones. Stopping to consider whether you should run away, when confronted by a predator, may not give you much of an advantage over an unconscious and automatic reflex to do so!

In considering the way in which evolution works, what is important is not so much what the mind is, but what it *does*. In other words, the mind is to be examined in terms of its function, and, indeed, the same functions (e.g. taking action to avoid being eaten when confronted with a predator) can take many different forms in different creatures with different brain and nervous system configurations. So perhaps it would be far more useful – in this enlarged world of cognitive science – to consider minds by examining the way in which they function, rather than the particular type of brain that they use for that functioning. And this leads us in the direction of *functionalism*, a theory which has been particularly important in cognitive science.

Functionalism

Functionalism is a theory developed in the 1960s, particularly by Hilary Putnam (b. 1926), which became influential in cognitive science. It has had its critics, of course, notably John Searle, whose views we shall examine in the next section.

There are many different forms of functionalism, but what they have in common is that they consider the way in which the mind processes the inputs from the senses and responds in terms of its outputs. As we shall see, there are problems with this approach, not the least of which is seeing whether it does not sufficiently allow for the mind to initiate action, rather than simply respond to what the senses convey to it.

Functionalism allows that mental states are real; they cause us to respond to the experiences we receive. Not every response can be measured in terms of movement or language. For example, faced with a lion in the jungle, it might be a good policy to freeze, hoping that the lion will take no notice. Certainly, attempting to run away in such circumstances would be no use at all. Hence, the mental response to the fear is to do nothing. At one level, this cannot be observed or measured. Of course, there is always the possibility that a heart monitor can register fear even if not a single muscle is moved in flight. Functionalism looks at the nature of the stimulus and the response that we make to it – and sees the primary function of the mind as sorting out how to respond to each given stimulus (just like a computer processing data).

As we shall see in the next chapter, neuroscience is giving us an increasingly detailed map of how various parts of the brain correspond to physical and mental operations. But the problem for anyone wanting to claim that the mind is somehow the product of brain activity is that we simply do not know enough about how activity in the brain relates to our experiences. This is where functionalism comes to the rescue. From a functionalist point of view, there is no need to wait for a full analysis of brain activity before sorting out the function of a particular mental quality. Pain, for example, causes a physical reaction of curling up or flinching, as a result of the damage to tissue. Exactly how that is turned into the experience we call pain can be left to one side. Thus functionalists produce what amounts to functional charts of the mind – showing the various inputs and responses – but that chart does not have to correlate precisely with the firing of neurons in the brain. It does not matter where or how the function happens, merely that it happens.

Insight

Functionalism is less concerned with the physical make-up of the brain, and more with the complex set of operations that its complexity enables it to carry out. In other words, it sees your mind as what your brain *does*, not what it *is*.

Whether or not conscious mental activity can be adequately described from a functionalist standpoint, one thing is absolutely clear: unconsciousness is the norm, consciousness the exception. The unconscious aspect of brain activity is constantly monitoring and adjusting our physical systems. If we get too hot, the pores or our skin open and release sweat; if we run up hill, more oxygen is needed, out heart beats faster and we gasp for breath. From resisting infection to emptying the bladder, the necessary actions to maintain our bodies are carried out on a functional basis – a need is registered and a responding action is taken.

Mostly, we run on autopilot; only occasionally do we have to make a conscious decision about what to do. But all that unconscious activity, constantly monitoring and adjusting our systems, might just as well be carried out be a suitably programmed computer – what matters is not so much what carries out the function as long as *something* does. In other words, the same function can be realized using different means.

As we shall see, this approach not only created a whole new way of describing how the mind works, it also opened up the possibility that mental operations could be realized using different physical means – and hence that a computer, assessing inputs and ordering responses, could be said to be conscious, intelligent even. But before we look at the issues with such a claim, we need to recognize another key feature of functionalism, namely that it avoided 'Leibniz's gap'.

GETTING ROUND THE 'GAP'?

Functionalism is one way to get around Leibniz's gap (see Chapter 2), by which there is always a gap between our description of a thought or cognition and our description of the electrochemical processes in our sensory organs and brain which correspond to it. In other words, the problem of not being able to describe thought in physical terms. Functionalism allows something to be described in terms of what it does, without having to specify exactly *how* it does it, or *what physical form it takes*.

Example

A bottle opener can take many forms. You can have the basic corkscrew with a simply handle for pulling upwards. There are more elaborate versions that have twin levers to pull the cork up, or those with a single lever to pull it from the side. Some corkscrews simply require the user to keep turning in the same direction: once the screw is fully within the cork, the same movement extracts it from the bottle. At one time it was popular to have a hollow needle with a pump on the end, extracting the cork through compressed air. And, of course, within the world of bottles there are some that have caps rather than corks. These can be prised off with a variety of openers. Some bottle tops can simply be unscrewed by hand – so perhaps the human hand can also be classified as a bottle opener!

Clearly, there is no single description to cover all bottle openers; the only thing these things have in common is their function.

It is therefore realistic to expect that we should be able to speak of a mental function, without having to describe the mechanics through which it works. From a functionalist perspective, a computer that performs an operation that in a human being would be described as the result of thinking is actually 'thinking'. But that does not in any way mean that the function is carried out in the same way and using the same mechanism in the computer and in the human brain.

Even if pain is real, pain is not exactly the same thing as the firing of neurons that takes place while the damage is being sustained and the resulting flinch is taking place. Rather, the brain activity and the subsequent bodily movements are the vehicle through which the pain is realized. Most functionalists are therefore content to say that there is no separate material basis for mind. The sort of causes of things that we call mental are realized in those ordinary physical circuits or structures.

The key question is whether this functionalist account of the mind has managed to get round Leibniz's gap. In other words, does functionalism allow you to say that mind and matter are different but equally real, neither being reduced to the other (in other words, avoiding either materialism or idealism) but able to interact?

My personal view on this is that:

▶ Functionalism does not fit well with a Cartesian substance dualism, since it describes mental functions in terms of a single chain of physical stimulus and response. It does not describe the mental as other than a function of the physical, so it never encounters a 'gap' that needs to be crossed.
▶ However, it fits better with property dualism, since the mental features it describes are not simply identified with particular physical features, but are realized *through* the physical. In

other words, in describing a physical process or function, I am introducing a new level of significance, to which mental attributes apply. So, for example, pain is real; it is not inserted into an otherwise material sequence of response to tissue damage, but is a way of describing that whole sequence.

Artificial intelligence

The idea of artificial intelligence (AI) becomes possible once thought is seen as a matter of computing – sorting out bits of information fed into the system by the senses. This is not a new idea; in fact it was put forward by Thomas Hobbes (1588–1679), who claimed 'Reasoning is but reckoning' (*Leviathan*, 1651). With this view, many of the problems associated with the dualist view of minds and bodies no longer apply. Thought is not occult or unknowable, but an operation performed on information provided by the senses. Although Hobbes saw mental activity as a material process, the implications of his approach have been appreciated only since the latter part of the 20th century with the advent of computers that are able to perform actions which resemble what a human being does when he or she 'thinks'. The issue of whether that physical process can simply be identified with thought and consciousness will be considered later, as it is absolutely crucial for the whole of the philosophy of mind.

Insight

From the 17th century you have the great divide between Descartes (and the whole Continental rationalist and idealist tradition that stemmed from his work) on the one hand, and the English empirical tradition on the other, typified by Locke and Hume. Hobbes, a forerunner of that latter tradition, saw our perceptions as nothing but stimuli on our sense organs. That view fitted well with empiricism, and with Locke's claim that the mind is a tabula rasa, waiting to be filled with information from the senses.

Almost all the discussions of the mind/body problem through until the mid-20th century – and the perception of the problem itself, come to that – was based on, or reacted to, the Cartesian approach. How different things might have been if the debate had stemmed from Hobbes.

A crucial further step needed to be taken before AI could be created. It came in the form of the theory of logic, developed by George Boole (1815–64). He saw thinking and logic as a matter of symbol manipulation, and also that any complex argument or process could be broken down into its constituent parts. Complex truths were in theory reducible in this way to binary truth-values – everything, in the last analysis, was a matter of yes/no or off/on. The implication of this is that complex concepts and arguments can be built up by the addition of very large numbers of basic binary choices.

A computer is a machine that operates a formal system of logical operations. It manipulates data according to a set of instructions. Basically, it has an input device to feed data, a processor that determines what shall be done with each incoming piece of information, and suitable output devices, depending on what the computer is required to do.

Similar processes

If you find it difficult to equate the artificial process that goes on in a computer memory with the working of the mind, consider the material basis of both. The computer works on a binary sequence, comprising a huge number of individual 'off/on' switches, which in turn switch others off or on. Individually, their significance is not apparent, but cumulatively they form the computer program and data, revealing and processing information at a level very far removed from the basic switches.

The brain goes through a similar process. Individual neurons either fire or do not fire (in other words, the follow the same 'off/on' pattern) and in turn cause many others to either fire or not fire. The process of thought only appears, at a physical level, through the operation of very large numbers of neurons – although, of course, the physical process by which the switching takes place is very different, and the plasticity and sheer complexity of the brain makes the analogy with the computer rather crude.

The fundamental question 'Can computers think?' was raised by Alan Turing (1912–54). He presented computers with a basic challenge, namely that they should be able to respond to questions in such a way that a person would not be able to know whether those answers were coming from a computer or another person – in other words, that they responded intelligently. This became known as 'the Turing Test', and it raises a whole range of questions, not just about AI, but about the nature of human cognition, and the relationship between 'mind' and 'brain'.

Insight

As we shall see below, the view that computation can be intelligent is challenged by John Searle in his well-known 'Chinese Room' thought experiment. The computer only appears to be intelligent because it has been programmed by an intelligent human being. Hence there is the danger of ascribing intelligence to a machine that is simply carrying out instructions in a mechanical way.

Thus, for example, if you have a human being and a computer playing chess, both are performing the same functions. Both are following a set of rules about how moves are to be made. The basic difference between them is that the human brain has many *other* things to do at the same time – from adjusting blood pressure to wondering about the next meal. But that is only a matter of complexity, and it could be argued that, in each of those functions, it is similarly following rules, just like the computer.

From the point of view of AI, the problem is therefore reversed. It is not a matter of asking how a computer can have a 'mind', but of why we need to think of a human as having a 'mind' over and above the various operations that it performs through the functioning of its brain. Are we not, in that sense, computers – with our various input and output devices (our senses and creative activities) and the firing of neurons (in the central processor unit between our ears) being the means by which we relate the one to the other?

Of course, one crucial difference between the responses of a computer and a human being is that the inputs and outputs of the human being have meaning or significance; they are not impersonal. The human being has a reason for doing what he or she does. In other words, human thought is a semantic formal system (a process that operates logically, and which also expresses meaning).

Insight

Functionalism fits well with AI simply because, for functionalists, mental operations are activities that can be performed in a number of different physical contexts, much the same way as a computer program can be run on different kinds of hardware. For functionalism, mental activity is a form of software, not part of the hardware that is running it. One could therefore examine mental functioning without having to have detailed information about the brain and its method of operation.

What then is the essential difference between the human being and the computer? Some possibilities were clearly set out by John Haugeland in his book *Semantic Engines: An introduction to mind design* (MIT Press, 1981). He suggests that those who claim that computers are essentially different from humans take one of two general lines of argument:

1 **The 'hollow shell' argument.** This suggests that semantic engines (i.e. computers that appear to use meaningful symbols) are not intelligent, but merely act 'as if' they are. They are a fake or a 'hollow shell' because they lack a special something that is required for real thought. That 'special something' could be:
   ▶ *consciousness* – although it is very difficult to specify what consciousness is
   ▶ *original intentionality* – in other words, the computer is programmed, but the human acts for his or her own reasons.
   ▶ *caring* – the computer does not have any concern about what is being processed, whereas the human being is committed and concerned about the things thought about, and can have very powerful emotional reactions to them.
2 **The 'poor substitute' argument.** This suggests that computers are good at doing a limited range of tasks, but that they will never become powerful enough to be able to get near what we know of human intelligence, or have anything like the range of abilities that we associate with common sense.

These arguments can be challenged:

▶ Since Haugeland's book was written, computer power has increased enormously. Children now play with computers many times more sophisticated than anything available in the 1980s. Might that process continue indefinitely? If so, can the 'poor substitute' argument hold?

- Notice also that consciousness, intentionality, emotional involvement and commitment are all very difficult to define, but may actually be programmable. Indeed, education and society aims at increasing social and emotional awareness. Is that not a case of programming for intentionality and emotional involvement? If so, apart from the quantity of computing power available within the human brain, and the range and scope of the input stimuli from birth onwards, which informs the growth of the intelligence and consciousness, what is the difference between human and computer?
- The whole process of child development, as explored within psychology, to say nothing of the problems of psychopathology, show ways in which thought and feeling later in life may be influenced by childhood experiences. The youthful computer is programmed (or rather, programmes itself – a point we shall look at later in terms of neural networks) by its experiences.
- If programming does not work, how do we account for the phenomena of hypnosis or most obviously NLP (Neuro-Linguistic Programming)? Therapy assumes that a programme may be examined and improved, changing the way in which the 'personality' responds to stimuli.

None of these points can prove that our brains are simply computers, but they suggest that it is difficult – from a functionalist perspective – to show the fundamental difference between the one and the other, other than in their degree of complexity.

FUNCTIONALISM AND AI

In general, the functionalist approach sees mental operations as being like the software that is running on the computer, while the brain itself is the hardware. This enables a clear distinction to be made between the formal operations (following the commands of the program), the semantic content (information that is being processed) and the material base that is supporting this function (the brain or computer memory). One thinker who has been particularly influential in presenting mental processes as computational and formal is Jerry Fodor (b. 1935). He argues for multiple realization – in other words, that the same mental states could exist in different complex systems. If a mental state can be expressed in brain matter, why not in its silicon equivalent?

This has implications for the mind/body relationship. We can appreciate that a computer program is not *part of* the hardware, but it does not operate *except as embodied in the hardware*. Also, the work of the computer is carried out as a result of actual electrical impulses in its memory, but that does not *exclude* the program from being the cause of what is being done. To say that an action is carried out either by the memory or by the program is just an example of what Ryle called the 'category mistake'.

If the mind is not just a result of physical activity in the brain, but actually causes it (as the program that is running causes particular sequences of activity within the computer memory), where does that mind '*come from*'?

Clearly, there are some interesting possibilities here. Does it come from social conditioning? Here we get into issues of language and how concepts are learned. By some kind of genetic inheritance? This leads us to consider if there are any innate ideas, rather than ideas that come to us as a result of what is conveyed by the senses.

Comment

AI does not, it seems to me, contribute a great deal to the issue of understanding the nature of human consciousness. If we could construct a human being with a brain and sensory system, with the ability to express itself as humans do, then it would be indistinguishable from a human being – and we would be no further forward. We would be no more able to examine the nature of its consciousness than we are that of any human being now.

All it could show is that there is no *separate mental substance*. But (sorry, Descartes) most of us knew that already!

We have here yet another example of an issue that bedevils the philosophy of science. Analysis does not, in itself, show the nature and operation of complex entities. In other words, you cannot understand the nature of a motoring holiday by a careful analysis of the various bits and pieces that go to make up a car engine. We cannot claim (as some of those engaged in AI appear to) that one day, when we have an absolutely 100-per-cent knowledge of every bit of that car, such that we can build an identical model from scratch, we will then have a complete sense of what the motoring holiday is about. The perfectly understood and reproduced car will tell us no more about that than does the present one. Analysis can be a dead end.

There is also a danger of circularity. A human mind devises a program for a computer, and is then surprised that the program works just like a human mind!

AI AND NEURAL COMPUTING

So far we have considered AI in terms of the functions of computers that are programmed to receive and respond to stimuli. But is that how human beings actually operate? Clearly, it is not. There is no point at which a young brain is programmed; it learns things gradually as it goes along. No two people have exactly the same mind, since no two people have had the same experience that have shaped their thinking or their values. People programme themselves.

'Neural computing' is the term used for the development of computers that can learn for themselves, rather than being programmed. In this, it is the conscious attempt to get a physical device to 'grow' a mind, in the same way as a human being.

The difference between these two forms of computing illustrates a feature of Ryle's argument in *The Concept of Mind*. Ryle distinguished between 'knowing that' and 'knowing how'. The former is the information that you have been fed by the senses; the latter is the awareness of how to perform some action. AI tends to concentrate on getting computers to 'know that' and to come up with the appropriate responses as a result. Neural computing tries to produce computers that will 'know how'.

Ryle speaks of the 'intellectualist legend', which is the idea that when someone wants to perform an intelligent task, he or she first of all has to think of all the rules involved, and then apply them. That, of course, is exactly what a computer does, since all the rules have been ready programmed into its memory. Rather, Ryle argues that intelligent action is a matter of instinctively knowing what one wishes to do in a situation, irrespective of any rules.

Neural networks offer the possibility that, one day, computers might be able to learn from new situations, and might therefore become creative. Every time something happens to a human being, that experience enters his or her memory, and will contribute to future decisions. 'I won't do that again!' or 'I'd like some more of that!' is the key to learning.

If minds were programmed, we'd all end up with a common set of values and assumptions about life. As it is, the ever-present possibility of becoming warped, damaged or inspired by life ensures that we remain remarkably different.

How exactly neural networking in the computer world might simulate the process of human learning is a technical matter, and the production of machines that can learn with anything like the sophistication of the human mind is far in the future, if indeed it ever becomes possible. For our purposes, however, it does highlight a major problem with conventional AI, and points out the engaged and ever-learning features of human minds. In *The Emperor's New Mind* (1989) Professor Roger Penrose of Oxford argued that it would be impossible to create an intelligent robot because consciousness requires self-awareness, and that is something a computer cannot simulate. It was a very serious attack on some of the rather naive and optimistic claims of those working in the field of artificial intelligence, but it does not really address the possibility of a computer which can learn, develop its own personal history, and thus create its own form of individual self-awareness.

world, relate to the experiences we have? Why do people sometimes change their views as they get older? Why do the minds of those with degenerative disease become so diminished? Why do drugs alter a person's mood or perception?

It is really inconceivable that the mind could be other than intimately related to the whole human organism and its world? To attempt to separate it off, making it a detached, non-extended substance, makes nonsense of everything from the desire to relax over a social drink, to the 'high' that comes from a good exercise session.

We are not minds loosely attached to bodies; we are *thinking and feeling beings*. Of all the areas in the philosophy of mind that illustrate this, the debate over AI perhaps makes it clearest, for the attempt to 'import' a mind and load it on to a machine is no more than a caricature of a truly thinking and feeling being.

THE INFINITE BACKGROUND PROBLEM

An additional problem here is raised by a philosopher who has nothing whatever to do with artificial intelligence – Martin Heidegger (1889–1976). He was an existentialist philosopher, concerned with the way in which people choose what to do, understand themselves, and live in an authentic way. One feature of his thinking about this is that we are 'thrown' into life at a particular time and place and that most of the circumstances we have to deal with are already given and not of our own choosing. In order to understand any choice, therefore, one needs to know something of the circumstances in which it is being made. But those circumstances are determined by yet other factors, and those by others still. Equally, the way we respond to situations is influenced by our own personal history, since memory plays a vital role in choosing how we are to act.

So there is a theoretically infinite background of facts that would need to be taken into account in order to fully understand even the most straightforward of choices. But, more than that, we do not just *observe* a world, we are *engaged* with it. Everything we do relates to our personal history and the society within which we live, everything is loaded with value and meaning for us. It therefore becomes nonsense to assume that you can isolate some particular bit of experience, program it into a computer and expect a response that would mirror what a real, engaged human being would do.

This tends to complicate the functionalist argument – since it is not simply a matter of processing a particular input data and coming up with a response. The mind takes into each decision its own history, and where it is responding to language, we need also to be aware that the person speaking or writing also has his or her own infinite background, and so on.

Thus the image of the mind as a basic machine within information being fed into it in a linear way, and a succession of outputs at the other, is very limited. In reality, there is a complex network of meanings, values and significances – a network that stretches out in all directions beyond even those things of which we are directly aware.

Insight

If we could construct a computer with the power of the human brain, fit it into the skull of a robot with the size, flexibility and functionality of a human body, allow it to grow (and thereby experience change) over a period of a human lifetime and surround it by a social and intellectual environment from which it can learn, we might end up with something quite amazing – an artificially constructed human being. Unfortunately, we would then have a problem – very similar to the one we have now – of understanding exactly how its artificial mind is related to its artificial body and artificial environment.

AI appears to work only because it is a simplified and limited version of the real thing. Real minds have an infinite background, and cannot therefore be artificially reproduced unless you have infinite time and infinite resources.

The 'Chinese Room'

One of the most important challenges to the scope of AI and the assumption that a computer program is in some way the equivalent of a mind was put forward in 1980 by the American philosopher John Searle (b. 1932). He set out to consider whether or not it was correct to say that a computer could actually understand (as opposed to manipulate) information, taking as his starting point the usual description of a computer as a 'formal symbol manipulation system'. In other words, the computer is programmed with a range of symbols and rules, and it follows these in order to produce its output.

He distinguished first of all between a 'weak' view of AI, which simply claims that AI is of value for helping us understand the way in which the mind works, and a 'strong' view, that a computer program is in fact a 'mind' and that it has cognitive states. It is this 'strong' view that Searle sets out to challenge.

He does so by considering our ability to understand stories. When a person is told a story in a language he or she knows, the person can understand that story and respond correctly when questions are asked. But if you don't know the language, you can't understand the story, and are quite unable to respond to questions.

Now, Searle considers the situation of a person who knows absolutely no Chinese. He is locked in a room and given a batch of Chinese writing. None of the characters mean anything to him. Then he is given a second batch, along with a set of instructions in English. These instructions help him to relate the second batch of characters to the first one.

Now, the first set represents a story in Chinese, and the second a set of potential questions and answers about it. The English instructions effectively link one set to another, so that the person can match up one character with another without needing to understand anything of what they actually mean.

A set of questions in Chinese is then fed into the room. Following the instructions, the person inside matches up the appropriate Chinese characters and posts out the required answer. If the instructions are followed correctly, a Chinese speaker on the outside will be receiving answers which would suggest that the person inside the room is able to read Chinese, understand the story and respond appropriately. But, of course, he actually understands not a word.

Searle's argument is that exactly the same thing is happening in the computer, in the situation that, according to the Turing Test, would suggest that a computer is thinking. The computer actually understands nothing.

Searle looks at the claims of AI, and comes to the conclusions that, just as he can manipulate Chinese characters without understanding them, so a computer can manipulate a set of formal symbols without actually knowing anything at all of what they stand for. All the computer has done is regurgitate what the programmer has put into it; it has not actually known anything, nor been aware of the significance of its operation. *In other words, it has not been 'thinking'.*

Searle is asking that those who suggest that 'strong' AI is possible (i.e. that you can create a computer which actually has a mind) should be able to say exactly what distinguishes mental from non-mental. If the answer is that a machine has a mind if its responses are intelligible, then his 'Chinese room' argument proves that false – for the man in the room has no knowledge of Chinese, although appearing to respond intelligently.

Towards the end of the argument, Searle makes two important points that link AI to the theories of mind that we have been considering earlier:

1 That the traditional test of an 'intelligent response' for deciding if a computer can think is effectively both behaviourist and operationalist. In other words, it is decided only upon what can be observed, not upon any direct awareness of the process of thought.
2 That it assumes a dualism of programs and hardware (with the programme seen as the 'mind' and the hardware upon which it runs as the 'brain') but that dualism separates the mind from its material matrix. True, it is not exactly the same dualism that was proposed by Descartes, but it certainly cuts out the possibility of a direct description of the mental in physical terms.

To the traditional question 'Can machines think?', his answer is 'Yes' – but only very special machines, namely human brains. He concludes:

'If mental operations consist in computational operations on formal symbols, then it follows that they have no interesting connection with the brain; the only connection would be that the brain just happens to be one of the indefinitely many types of machines capable of instantiating the program. ... AI has little to tell us about thinking, since it has nothing to tell us about machines. By its own definition, it is about programs, and programs are not machines. Whatever else intentionality is, it is a biological phenomenon, and it is as likely to be as causally dependent on the specific biochemistry

> **of its origins as lactations, photosynthesis or any other biological phenomena.'**
>
> From *Minds, Brains and Programs*, as reproduced in R. Cummins and D.D. Cummins (eds), *Minds, Brains and Computers*, p. 151 (a further version of this was included in Searle's 1984 Reith Lectures, 'Minds, Brains and Science')

In other words, the process of cognition and intentionality (acting with purpose) is a phenomenon of a whole organism. It is linked to what it means biologically to be a human being, and therefore it cannot be equated with a programmed set of instructions in the brain.

But it remains a possibility for Searle that neuroscience might one day be able to give an account of the brain that would explain how consciousness is caused, and that would (for him) finally overcome the mind/body problem.

A key feature of Searle's approach, brought out very clearly in his book *The Rediscovery of Mind* (1992) is that it was always a mistake to assume that something is either mental or physical, but that it cannot be both at the same time:

> **'The brain causes certain "mental" phenomena, such as consciousness mental states, and these conscious states are simply higher-level features of the brain.**
>
> **The fact that a feature is mental does not imply that it is not physical; the fact that a feature is physical does not imply that it is not mental.'**
>
> *The Rediscovery of Mind*, p. 14

Searle is making a crucially important point here. It he is right, much of what has been done in the philosophy of mind is simply mistaken, since it has been based on invalid assumptions.

Searle's position seems to be a form of property dualism, since his 'higher-level' description of a physical process is simply describing it in a different way (namely, a holistic way) from that of the reductive analyst, who is concerned only with the lower levels. However, the difference between Searle's position and that of a property dualism approach is that, for Searle, there is a single reality that is multi-layered, and our language reflects that multi-layering. This is not quite the same as saying that a single reality may be *described* in two different ways, since it implies that *the layering is a feature of reality, not just of language.*

Searle therefore introduces 'concept dualism' (as an alternative to 'substance dualism' or 'property dualism'). A concept can refer to something physical or to something mental, but not to both. What he is concerned to maintain is the standard scientific way of looking at the material world, alongside the indisputable fact of consciousness:

> 'What I want to insist on, ceaselessly, is that one can accept the obvious facts of physics – for example, that the world is made up entirely of physical particles in fields of force – without at the same time denying the obvious facts about our own experiences – for example, that we are all conscious and that our conscious states have quite specific irreducible phenomenological properties. (The fact that a feature is mental does not imply that it is not physical; the fact that a feature is physical does not imply that it is not mental.)'
>
> The Rediscovery of Mind, p. 28

In other words, you don't have to choose between materialism and some form of dualism, whether as presented by the older debates or in the new context of cognitive science. You can – and should – have the best of both worlds.

10 THINGS TO KEEP IN MIND

1 Cognitive science is a multidisciplinary attempt to understand the mind, originating in the mid-20th century. It aims at a scientifically based approach to questions previously considered only by philosophy.

2 Psychology explores the relationship between the mind and physical expression, with behaviourists identifying the two.

3 Chomsky thought we have innate capabilities for the acquisition of language.

4 Wittgenstein claimed in *Tractatus Logico-Philosophicus* that the self was not in but was the *limit* of the world as verified by sense experience.

5 Evolutionary psychology looks at the biological advantage given by having a mind.

6 Functionalism examines the process of sensory inputs and responses.

7 AI explores the parallels between the operation of minds and computers.

8 AI is functionalist.

9 Neural computing explores how computers can learn.

10 Searle showed that you can manipulate characters without understanding them.

4

Physicalism and neuroscience

In this chapter you will:
- *examine physicalist / materialist approaches to mind*
- *consider the difference between eliminative and non-reductive materialism*
- *explore the contribution of neuroscience.*

> *'"I am body and soul" – so speaks the child. And why should one not speak like children?*
>
> *But the Awakened, the enlightened man says: I am body entirely, and nothing beside; and soul is only a word for something in the body.*
>
> *The Body is a great intelligence, a multiplicity with one sense, a war and a peace, a herd and a herdsman.*
>
> *Your little intelligence, my brother, which you call "spirit", is also the instrument of your body, a little instrument and toy of your great intelligence.*
>
> *You say "I" and you are proud of this word. But greater than this – although you will not believe it – is your body and its great intelligence, which does not say "I" but performs.'*
>
> Friedrich Nietzsche, *Thus Spoke Zarathustra*

In many areas of philosophy, religion and politics, Friedrich Nietzsche (1844–1900) anticipated later debates, and that is, in part, why he is one of the most fascinating thinkers of the 19th century. His comments quoted above are from a section of Zarathustra entitled 'On the despisers of the body'. In this section he appears to be attacking those who hold a dualistic position for primarily religious reasons, and who therefore tend to demote the body.

He anticipates behaviourism and the linguistic analysis of language about the self, by saying that the soul is 'only a word for something in the body', and also brings together more recent thinking about the role of the mind and its relationship with emotions and those drives that are based on the promptings of hormones, by pointing out that the mind is both 'herd and herdsman'. In other words, that in some way the mind embraces all the dynamic elements within the body, but also has the role of controlling and directing them. His idea of the 'great intelligence' therefore appears to embrace both rationality and emotion, both conscious and unconscious. It is not merely the self that identifies itself as 'I', but the 'I' that operates as an independent entity. We shall return to this later, in considering the instrumentalist approach to mind.

In this section, we shall therefore be looking at some approaches which, like Nietzsche, set aside the dualism of Descartes by eliminating the need for a separate mental substance – seeing the mind as a feature of the body, and language about the mind as being a convenient way of describing actual or anticipated bodily actions.

In general, therefore, a materialist or physicalist approach (meaning the same thing, the latter becoming the more fashionable term recently) is one that claims that mental phenomena can be explained in terms of, or reduced to, physical phenomena. Partly as a result of work in the cognitive sciences, but also as part of a general philosophical retreat from dualistic and religious thinking, a majority of philosophers today seem to adopt the physicalist approach to mind. However, as we shall see, there are significant problems with this approach – and particularly with the view that neuroscience (although hugely important and valuable medically) will somehow answer all the traditional questions about the mind and its relationship to the body, or about the nature of persons.

'Is'

In any situation where two things – in the case of materialism, thought and brain processes – are identified, it is important to distinguish between the 'is' of definition and the 'is' of composition. Thus, for example, a symphony 'is' merely a set of vibrations in the air. It is *composed of* those vibrations, and without those vibrations, no symphony. On the other hand the meaning of 'vibrations in the air' and 'symphony' are quite different. The symphony cannot sensibly be *defined as* vibrations in the air, even if it is composed of them.

We need to be aware that some of the objections that are raised to a materialist view are based on the assumption that, once you have an identity of composition, it automatically follows that you have an identity of definition.

In other words, if my thoughts are 'nothing but' brain processes (in the sense of being composed of those and no other phenomena), then it follows that thoughts are 'the same thing as' brain processes, which is obvious nonsense. What happens in the grey matter between our ears is nothing like the sensations of colour or sound, or the emotions and thoughts that are experienced.

Thomas Hobbes was concerned to understand the nature of perception. He argued that external objects exerted physical pressure on our sense organs and that these physical effects were mediated by nerves to the mind and heart. There they take on the appearance of being qualities in the external body. But Hobbes holds that they are in fact *a matter of fancy*; in other words, that they are mental constructs. And he holds that this must be the case, since physical movement can only cause other physical movement.

Hence, whatever is the cause of our sense experience can only cause physical activity in the heart and mind, not what we experience as sensations, which are clearly non-physical. Thus, although we think that our concept (fancy) actually applies to the external object, nevertheless the object is one thing, the image or fancy is another.

In a sense, this leads Hobbes to the kind of 'internal theatre' view of the mind, although he also makes careful the distinction between the mind that assembles such 'fancies' and the physical basis of consciousness, which is part of an ongoing chain of physical causes and effects.

For Hobbes therefore, even perception is part of the mechanical, physical world, and – rather like the epiphenomenal approach – what we term 'mind' builds upon it. And, of course, with the triumph of Newtonian science, everything came to be seen in terms of the interaction of physical bodies, moved by forces that operated in terms of the laws of physics.

A materialist approach therefore need not deny that there are mental states; it simply says that to have a mental state is simply what happens when a particular brain state is taking place. So, to take the most common example, pain is a real, conscious experience – but it is simply what happens when there is a certain pattern of activity in your brain and nervous system, resulting from damage to the body.

Insight

We cannot doubt conscious experiences any more than Descartes could doubt himself as a thinking being, and for the same reason – the act of doubting presupposes the very thing it attempts to doubt. The question is whether that experienced process is *anything other than* what we can describe in terms of activity in the brain and nervous system. Materialists do not argue that mental states do not exist, simply that they are nothing other than brain states. In other words, they reject the idea of a secondary mental 'substance' of the sort that Descartes accepted.

There is good evidence to suggest that the mind is, in some way, a feature of the brain. For example, a person suffering severe depression can be helped by having ECT treatment, which involves giving the brain electric shocks, simulating epileptic fits. Equally, a person who suffers brain damage may become a changed character. It is also possible to monitor every human activity in terms of physical movements brought about by electrochemical activity in muscles, nerves and brain. It can always be seen as a self-contained process, involving electrochemical and mechanical components, with no 'gap' into which the mind can insert itself. But, if there seems no point at which the mind intervenes in that chain of causes, why do we need to think in terms of a mind at all?

In general, materialism takes a reductionist approach to mental activity; a person is seen as 'nothing but' a brain, attached to a body and nervous system. The 'nothing but' distinguishes materialism from more subtle forms of dualism. Nobody would deny that, in some sense, a mind is closely linked to a brain and nervous system; the problem is to express what a 'something more' might be, if the materialist position seems inadequate.

Even if the materialist and reductionist position is correct, that need not hinder our discussion of 'mental' concepts, for it would be as unreasonable to abandon speaking about the mind, just because we know it to be the firing of neurons in the brain, as to abandon speaking about Mozart simply because we know his music is nothing by vibrations in the air.

Behaviourism

In psychology, behaviourism developed out of the frustration of trying to find something that could be observed and monitored, as opposed to sensations, which were known only through introspection and could not be assessed objectively. Behaviourism is a materialist/physicalist theory, in that it reduces 'mental' concepts, such as having a pain or being happy, to physical activity. For a behaviourist, crying out and rubbing the damaged part of the body is exactly what 'being in pain' is about. There is no separate or private activity going on, over and above the physical, and publicly observable, behaviour.

Ivan Pavlov (1849–1936) in Russia, J.B. Watson (1875–1958) and B. Fred Skinner (1904–90) in the USA were hugely influential in their day. Their work was based on measuring physical responses to stimuli. Indeed, the term 'Pavlovian reaction' is commonly used to describe an immediate and 'unthinking' response.

Pavlov, for example, would monitor a dog's salivation at the sight or anticipation of food, and then explore ways in which it might be trained to expect food if it performed a particular action. Skinner is remembered for his rats in cages. Behaviourists generally worked in laboratories, watching the way in which animals learned to do simple tasks, such as pressing a switch in the hope of getting food.

This approach to studying the mind may seem very limited, considering the range of views that we have considered so far, but one should keep in mind that *the aim of behaviourism was to produce a science of mind, with results that could be measured and evaluated.* The measurement of behaviour in response to stimuli represent the only such measurable data – so it was quite natural that behaviour should be seen as the key to find what was happening in the mind.

In general, the behaviourists saw the task of psychology as predicting and controlling behaviour, and they saw the key to that in environment and stimuli. Our activity is not decided by some private activity going on in the mind, but by our conditioned responses to the environment.

The political agenda

A behaviourist approach considers people to be shaped primarily by their environment (they are simply responding to their circumstances) and is therefore likely to consider people primarily as products of their particular background, class and so on. Both Watson and Skinner defined the aim of psychology as the prediction and control of behaviour. The behaviourist approach therefore had enormous implications for society and education. If minds were simply responses to stimuli, then controlling the environment would shape the thought and attitude. This was in radical contrast to the traditional dualist view that the mind was independent of the body, and could therefore in some measure transcend its environment.

It is almost impossible to overemphasize the importance of this distinction between traditional dualism and behaviourism – so much in terms of the politics, the philosophy and the culture of the 20th century was shaped by what was, in effect, the issue about whether individuals have unique, independent minds, or are the products of conditioning. Social engineering is a natural outcome of behaviourism.

The behaviourist's dilemma is as follows:

▶ You can't observe thought.
▶ Therefore any one account of the thought that gave rise to an action is as good as any other, since it is not open to verification of any sort.

▶ The behaviourist answer is to ignore thought and go for what can be observed – behaviour.

▶ But human behaviour is so complex, and so obviously related to overall views and goals, that it is impossible to give an adequate description of it (let alone an explanation) without a fair amount of interpretation, which presupposes issues, such as intention and purpose, that behaviourism was attempting to avoid.

Example

A person steps off the pavement and holds up their hand to stop the traffic. An oncoming vehicle stops, allowing a car to back out of a concealed drive into the road. The person then waves the vehicle on and mouths the word 'Thanks' to the driver.

▶ It is almost inconceivable that the ability to perform those actions could have been learned by trial and error! (How many times would he or she get knocked down before it worked?)

▶ It is possible that the person who stopped the car has never had to do so before, nor has the person ever had to back out of that drive into the road before.

▶ Stopping one's car when a person holds up their hand is straightforward – a rule to be learned.

▶ On the other hand, what of the sequence in which a person recognizes that it is a difficult turning to back out of; thinks that there is a danger of a collision; decides to go and stop the traffic; beckons the car out; acknowledges and thanks the driver who has stopped? Could each of these been learned by a process of stimulus and response?

▶ Is it not more likely that there are a sequence of private 'thoughts', imagining various scenarios and working out which of these are desirable (a safe journey) or not (getting hit when backing out), and then working out what needs to be done to secure the first rather than the second?

▶ It may be possible that basic behaviourism could go a long way to showing the stimulus-and-response basis for each part of that action. But the result would be very complex indeed. It is easier to posit some form of mental activity, even if it cannot be observed directly.

We need to distinguish two kinds of behaviourism. The approach described above may be termed *methodological behaviourism*, in that it simply relates input stimuli to the resulting behaviour. *Logical behaviourism* takes this a step further, suggesting that mental terms can be defined in terms of observable behaviour. For example, to have a pain *means* to grimace, to clutch the affected spot and so on. The best-known exponent of this approach is Gilbert Ryle (see Chapter 2).

In general, behaviourists described volitional concepts (e.g. wanting or intending things) and descriptions of personal attributes (e.g. being kind) in terms of *dispositions*. To say that someone is kind is simply to say that, in certain circumstances, they will have a general disposition to behave in ways that we sum up as being 'kind' – there is no inner, hidden quality of kindness.

Insight

The development of behaviourism as a philosophy of mind should be seen against the background of a more general movement in philosophy in the early 20th century – Logical Positivism. Inspired by the success of the sciences, and hoping to encourage language to have the kind of evidential precision required by science, this school of thought argued that the meaning of a statement was its method of verification. Without evidence, a claim becomes meaningless. Therefore the behaviourists were concerned that all mental claims should be explained in terms of physical evidence.

In the end, behaviourism fails to give an adequate account of the human experience of mind. It leaves out purpose and intention, and leaves little scope for insight and interpretation. Even if it avoids 'the ghost in the machine', it simply transfers the problem into one of 'the ghost in the action' – for the actions which display our dispositions need to be interpreted if we are to make sense of them. The important thing is often not *what* you do, but *why* you do it, and to this behaviourism had no convincing answer.

Eliminative materialism

Back in the 1950s, some philosophers were arguing that mental states were in fact identical to brain states, so that, for example, the feeling of pain is the firing of certain neurons in the brain. U.T.

Place, in an article entitled 'Is Consciousness a Brain Process?' published in the *British Journal of Psychology* in 1956, argued that explanations of introspective observations were made more difficult by the 'phenomenological fallacy' (see Chapter 6) – the mistaken idea our descriptions of things related to some mysterious internal environment. He considered that, once that fallacy was cleared away, it would be recognized that there was nothing an introspecting subject could say about his or her conscious experiences which 'is inconsistent with anything a physiologist might want to say about the brain processes which *cause* him or her to describe the environment and his consciousness of the environment in the way that he does.'

Insight

The word to notice here, which I have italicized but Place did not, is 'cause'. It is one thing to say that a mental process may be described in terms of brain activity – just as a walk might be described in terms of the movement of leg muscles – but quite another to suggest that the brain process *causes* consciousness or even the description of consciousness. It is a short step from that position to one which claims that our thoughts and intentions are controlled by our brains, with freedom of thought and action no more than a convenient illusion.

At the time, such a view was in the minority, but today some form of material identification of mental operations with brain activity is the norm, both among philosophers and neuroscientists. The most clear-cut approach to this is termed 'eliminative materialism', and claims that, when we speak of mental phenomena – thoughts, desires, emotions and so on – there is nothing that corresponds to those words, other than physical states. This approach, taken by the American philosophers Richard Rorty (b. 1931), Paul and Patricia Churchland (b. 1942 and 1943), Daniel Dennett (b. 1942) and others, makes what appears to be the implausible claim that mental states simply do not exist.

Eliminative materialists tend to argue that mental states, such as hoping, wishing, believing and so on, are part of a primitive way of thinking with which we have developed in order to predict what others will do – a 'folk psychology' – soon to be replaced by a direct examination of neural activity. However, it can be argued, on pragmatic grounds, that the 'folk' idea that we have mental states works perfectly well, and yields useful information about other people. It is also useful in seeing individuals as part of a wider network of communications and relationships. Therefore, it has much to recommend it as a theory to explain human behaviour. In my view, the fact that it is a common assumption, rather than an improbable academic theory, should count for rather than against it!

Insight

The argument goes that, if it were possible to give a complete account of brain activity (in other words, a perfect neurobiology), we would then have a complete explanation of brain functioning, and there would be no place within that explanation for things like beliefs or hopes.

Another significant aspect of eliminative materialism is that it is 'anti-foundationalist'; in other words, it argues that there is nothing inside us that we have not put there ourselves, and no fundamental principle of reason that is not simply a convention that we have chosen to use. That is to say, there are no transcendent or general foundations for 'mind', but merely the gathering together of what society offers.

There are obvious problems with this sort of position, not least of which is that it is obvious that we do have minds and we are conscious. Therefore, even if it can be shown that there is no mental or conscious activity that is not accompanied by brain activity, that does not necessarily mean that – at any level at which we can make use of the idea – the mind does not exist. So, for example, John Searle criticizes this approach in *The Rediscovery of Mind*. He argues that it is the equivalent of saying that a perfect theory of nuclear physics could explain all reality, and therefore that ordinary objects, like cars and golf clubs, therefore did not exist!

However, the significance of eliminative materialism is the degree to which it has fallen in awe of developments in neuroscience, and assumed that all other language about the mind is in some way pre-scientific. We shall look at neuroscience is a later section, but keep in mind that there were materialist views of the mind long before that branch of science managed to make visible the brain activity that inevitably corresponds to the workings of the mind.

NON-REDUCTIVE MATERIALISM

In the chapter on dualism, we took a brief look at 'property dualism', the view that mental properties were distinct from physical properties, even if they were dependent on them. It will be clear by now that this is also a form of materialism, although one which is not eliminativist (in that it allows the reality of the mind) or reductionist (in that it does not reduce the mental to the physical).

If mental properties are distinct from but dependent upon the physical, the crucial question is whether or not they can initiate or have any causal input into the physical:

▶ If they can't, you're back to a form of epiphenomenalism (see Chapter 2), which does not do justice to our experience of what minds achieve.
▶ If they can, you have to explain how it is that the mental can inject an additional cause into a physical world that already has a closed system of causes. In other words, if every physical action is already adequately accounted for in terms of physical causes, it is difficult to see where mental causation can fit in.

And so we are back to the problem of Descartes' pineal gland! The difference now is that the basic commitment is to a physicalist view of the world and the problem of how mental properties fit into it. Some physicalists seem prepared to say that neurons 'learn' things, or that brain activity takes place immediately before a decision is taken, thus suggesting that the conscious decision is merely an epiphenomenon. In doing so, they have effectively turned the whole of the brain into a Cartesian 'pineal gland' – in other words, the whole brain, with its billions of neurons and trillions of synaptic connections is the point at which mental properties come into play. *But this does not solve Descartes' problem; it merely restates it.* If you have different properties – some applied at the physical level, others at the mental – you still need to say whether there can be any 'top-down' causation (i.e. that the mental can affect the physical). If it can't, then we are effectively back to an eliminativist materialism with impotent mental descriptions attached. We shall examine this issue, in connection with free will and ethics, in Chapter 9.

A non-reductive materialism implies a *functionalist* account of the mind. Consciousness is not *identified* with grey matter, but is *expressed through* the patterns and operations that go on within it. And it is no more crazy to say that the mind is expressed through such patterns as it would be to say that a Mozart symphony is expressed through the various blowing and scrapings carried out by members of the orchestra. *Physical expression is not the same thing as reductionism.* Just as we do not have to ask where the symphony can be found, once all the instruments are playing, so we do not have to locate mind, once we are aware of the neural patterns that are operating in the brain.

Neuroscience

For a physicalist, matter is the only sort of stuff there is, and the mind therefore cannot be anything other than a physical phenomenon, subject – like everything else – to the laws of physics. This has become a contemporary orthodoxy, popularized by philosophers such as Daniel Dennett, and the starting point for most serious discussion of the mind. Just as the scientists of the 17th and 18th centuries claimed to have shaken off the shackles of superstition in order to judge everything according to reason and evidence, so modern physicalists claim to have freed the study of the mind from the older dualism of Descartes and religious concepts of the soul.

The one thing everyone seems agreed on is that the centre of operations for the mind is found in the brain. It's hardly a new idea; the early philosopher and medic Hippocrates (*c.*460– 377 BCE) considered the emotions to arise from the brain, and over the centuries the axe, guillotine and noose have effectively illustrated the inability of the body to maintain consciousness and life itself once deprived of the operations of its head!

Until recently, however, there was no way of observing the activity of a living brain. With neuroscience that has now changed. Functional Magnetic Resonance Imaging is able to see details of the soft tissues of the brain and also monitor the changes to the blood flow to various parts of the brain, indicating areas of neural activity.

There is no scope here even to start to describe the findings of neuroscience. It is a huge and important area of science, and has yielded amazing results both for medicine and for fundamental research into how the brain works. For the purpose of our discussion, however, certain features need to be kept in mind:

- We know that, although certain parts of the brain are associated with particular mental and conscious functions – sight, hearing, language, emotions and so on – activity in those parts goes alongside a more generalized level of activity elsewhere, and that, if part of the brain is disabled (e.g. though a stroke), other parts may be able to take over some of its functions.
- Hence we know that the brain is flexible, and that it can 'learn'. If we decide to take up playing a musical instrument, for example, or take a course in touch-typing, our brain will gradually respond and help us to achieve the manual dexterity we need. Things – whether physical or mental – become easier with practice.
- Most of what the brain does is concerned with the unconscious monitoring of the body's systems – blood pressure, temperature, and so on.
- We also know that, with billions of neurons, the brain is the most complex thing in the known universe. Our present attempts to monitor neural activity are relatively crude, in that they deal with large numbers of neurons working together, and generally see only what is happening after the event, in terms of the need for additional blood supplies.

If there is one thing we need to take from these four basic points it is this: the brain is not like a computer with a fixed amount of memory, a single-speed processor, or a preloaded set of programs. It is amazingly complex and flexible. It is not a crude physical machine that might just produce 'mind' as an epiphenomenon. If it is to be seen in terms of a machine at all, it is an extremely flexible one that has a two-way relationship with what we experience as mind.

Insight

This last point is crucial. If, through mental effort, we can actually change and streamline the neural pathways in the brain – shaping up our ability to do things, or enabling us to change our blood pressure or levels of anxiety through meditation, for example. Then the old divisions between dualism and materialism are inadequate. The brain cannot be a machine that happens to produce the illusion of mind; it is better thought of as the skill-centre of a living, thinking being.

In spite of the brilliant achievements of neuroscience to date, our understanding of how the brain works is in its relative infancy.

Indeed, philosophers who want to argue that neuroscience will provide all the answers to what we experience as mind tend to speak of a 'perfect neuroscience' in the future, rather than our present state of knowledge.

There are two basic questions we need to address here:

1 In what way (if at all) does the ability of neuroscience to observe neural functioning change the traditional question of how mind relates to body?
2 Would a perfect neuroscience render the idea of the mind redundant?

Nobody seriously doubts that the brain is the physical organ most immediately responsible for those things that we experience as mind. The fact that we can now 'see' the neural activity corresponding to consciousness and mind, only reinforces that point. But the brain is part of the physical world and subject to physical causation, and that fact does not change with the closer inspection of the brain that neuroscience provides. The old problem of how brain activity actually delivers the experience of consciousness, or how a mental operation (e.g. deciding to do something) can result in physical action, remains the same.

Hence, if a perfect neuroscience enabled us to observe the operation, over milliseconds, of the chemical exchanges and pulses of changed electrical potential that constitute the firing of each of the billions of neurons, that would not in itself solve the mind/body problem. It would simply give us a far more detailed picture of the body. We would still be left with the mystery of how all that detailed neural activity related to our conscious experience. Neurobiology examines the brain and nervous system. It looks at the way in which neurons take information from other neurons at their dendritic synapses, process it, and then send it out, through their axonal synapses, to other neurons. In other words – it looks at the biological systems *in which mental activity is realized.*

And, turning to the second question, there is one huge issue that neuroscience cannot address – namely that it is science, and therefore that it is the product of human minds! How is it possible for the mind to come to the conclusion that minds do not exist?

Psychology deals with the mind and neurobiology deals with the brain and nervous system. The key question (unanswerable at the moment) is whether, as neuroscience develops, these two disciplines will come together to give a single overall explanation of the brain/mind phenomenon? If so, it will be another case of *reductionism*, claiming that the mind is reduced to, or 'nothing but', brain states.

This extends what we already know, namely that alteration to the brain – whether through drugs or physical trauma, for example – can change personality. But that simply reinforces the unchallenged claim that the brain is the physical seat of the mind, it does not necessarily imply that we have no more use for language about the mind. Even if my mental condition requires the readjustment of my brain, that would not suggest that the condition and the brain were one and the same thing, merely that the latter was the physical locus of the former.

But there is another reason why we need to avoid a simple reductionist approach here. Returning to the discussion of evolutionary biology, we can ask: Why then has humankind developed such a large brain, compared with other species?

Clearly, the answer lies in the function that the brain and nervous system performs. Remembering things, communicating with others, solving puzzles, thinking how best to trap an animal or find other forms of food. All these things are mental – the more subtle the animal's thought processes and sensitive its consciousness of its environment, the more capable it will be of working out how best to survive, find food, compensate for its lack of strength and so on.

We observe the increase in time of the cranial capacity of hominids and conclude that the brain developed size and complexity because it enhanced the ability of individuals to survive. In other words – *it solved problems*. Hence, although we may not know *how* the brain succeeds in representing complex phenomena, we know *why* it does so.

But that basic fact highlights another – namely that, in order to understand the mind/brain, you need to see it *in its functional context*. What we experience as mind is all about the relationship that an individual has with his or her world; our experiences, emotions, thoughts, hopes and fears are all related to 'our world'. Whether they may also be tracked in terms of neural activity in our heads is a secondary matter.

Cities and stress

In a study carried out by a professor from the University of Heidelberg in Germany and published in 2011, healthy volunteers from rural and urban areas had their brains scanned while performing mental arithmetic tasks that were designed to make them feel anxious. The results showed that the amygdala (responsible for monitoring and responding to emotional and stressful situations) of those who lived in cities became overactive compared from the rural volunteers.

Notice the implication of this. The environment in which people normally live influences their brain's capacity to cope with and respond to stress. That suggests a very subtle relationship between how and where a person chooses to live and the way their brain develops to cope with what that involves. Neuroscience thus shows the physical correlate of what we can observe and experience – namely that life in cities can be stressful, and that too much stress can lead to anxiety and depression. The brain does not *cause* that situation, it *responds* to it.

What neuroscience has done is to make a crude 'substance' dualism untenable. It is quite unrealistic, in considering how the biological system has developed, or how the brain operates, to claim that the mind is utterly separate from the body. On the other hand, the complexity and flexibility of the brain shows that a crude, mechanical view of the self is equally inadequate. There are certainly functions and properties, applying to the whole individual in his or her world, that do not show up at the level of neurons firing, but which are no less real for that, and which have set the biological, evolutionary agenda for the development of the brain in the first place.

It is all too easy to get trapped into thinking that the only options are a full-blown dualism – with two separate substances and two sets of causes – or a reductionist materialism in which the mind is eliminated from the physical world. Yet everything we think or do presupposes and is dependent upon the mind, while everything we discover in science presupposes a universe of physical stuff. The key thing to keep in mind, as was pointed out by John Searle, is that for something to be mental does not imply that it is not also physical.

Insight

The philosophy of mind should not assume that neuroscience will solve its problems. Like any science, it is a mental discipline, using observation, analysis and logic to give a more detailed picture of the physical world. As such, neuroscience is an activity of the mind, attempting to explain how the brain relates to the mind. Brilliant thought it has been in terms of its technical and medical achievements, it is therefore open to all sorts of logical problems, and has certainly not solved the ongoing mind/body question.

10 THINGS TO KEEP IN MIND

1 Physicalism/materialism see the mind as a feature of the body.

2 Materialism tends to be reductionist.

3 Behaviourism measures responses to stimuli.

4 Eliminative materialism regards mind as simply a way of describing brain processes.

5 Eliminative materialists tend to describe ordinary language about minds as 'folk psychology'.

6 Non-reductive materialism is a form of 'property dualism'.

7 Neuroscience can show patterns of neural behaviour corresponding to mental operations.

8 The brain is flexible and responds to mental training.

9 Some claim that a perfect neuroscience would eliminate the need to speak of minds.

10 Neuroscience is itself a mental/intellectual activity.

5

Consciousness

In this chapter you will:
- *be conscious of the hard problem of consciousness*
- *consider whether you could be disembodied*
- *take an existentialist view.*

What does it mean to be conscious? How do I know that someone else is conscious? How is my conscious experience of things related to what is going on in my brain? Is disembodied consciousness possible?

It is one of the very worst features of philosophy that it can sometimes delight in making the obvious seem improbable. There have been many arguments outlined in this book that might suggest that consciousness does not really exist, or is really no more than a disposition to behave in a certain way. However, we know what it is to be conscious and to say that someone is conscious – in other words, we have an intuitive knowledge of consciousness. What is difficult is actually defining and explaining it. In particular, the really 'hard' problem is seeing how we can relate consciousness to the physical reality of what is happening in our brains.

Insight

Sometimes a hard problem may be caused by asking a wrong question. How is it that electrochemical activity in my brain can cause me to experience something as 'red'? Is that a valid question to which we do not yet know the answer? Or is the question itself wrong (in that it assumes a single causal series linking brain activity with conscious experience)? Does it assume what Ryle termed a 'category mistake' (see Chapter 2)?

Probably as good a starting point as any is to distinguish between simple consciousness and *reflective self-consciousness*. The latter is a human quality of being not only aware, but aware that one is aware: it allows a person to reflect, rather than just accept, his or her experiences and responses to them. However, consciousness itself operates also at a simpler, unreflective level, as awareness of the external world.

Consciousness is a feature of whole people not parts of them. In other words, it would seem inappropriate to say that the eye or the optic nerve was conscious, but if, as a result of the operation of the eye and the optic nerve, you can see and be aware of things around you, then *you* can be said to be conscious. Consciousness does not reside in the sense organs themselves, but is used to describe what is happening when the sense organs are transmitting information which is being processed, and to which a response can be given.

Insight

It is important to remember that your eye does not see, any more than your camera takes a photograph. *You* see and *you* take the photograph; the eye and the camera are simply the means by which you do so. It is essential to keep this distinction in mind, or we shall slip into the madness of thinking that our brains decide what we do, as though there were a separate little person (a homunculus) living inside our head.

Your consciousness does not depend on the degree of physical response you give to stimuli – after all, you could be conscious but paralysed – but we generally assume that there will be *some* response. If you lose consciousness, you cease to experience, but that can only be recognized by someone else if you stop responding to stimulus. After all, losing consciousness is one of the body's defence mechanisms against unbearable pain. That does not mean, of course, that your brain ceases to function – its many unconscious functions will continue for as long as you are alive; indeed, the cessation of brain activity is used as an indication of death in situations where bodily functions are being maintained artificially.

Qualia

'Qualia' is the term used for the basic 'phenomenal qualities' of experience – the taste of something, its colour or texture, the sound of a piece of music. Qualia are the building blocks of sentient life, the simplest elements of experience; we are aware of them all the time. However, it is very difficult to explain qualia, except in terms of other qualia or subjective experience as a whole. Why should it be that photons entering the eyeball cause me to see this particular thing? How is it possible for the neurons in my brain to enable me to see something as 'red'?

Qualia cause a problem for the functionalist approach to mind. If the mind is simply a processor that receives inputs and decides the appropriate responses (which is, crudely, what functionalism claims), then how does that process relate to what we actually experience? But qualia are a problem for any physicalist explanation of mind, for it is difficult to relate electrochemical activity in the brain, nervous system and sensory organs to 'what it is like' to have an experience, see a colour, enjoy a taste. The is the 'hard' problem of consciousness.

In an article in 1974, Thomas Nagel famously asked 'What is it like to be a bat?' The answer we give to that question is most significant, so let's reflect on it for a moment.

First of all, if we simply try to imagine that we (with our existing faculties) are living as a bat, then the situation seems quite bizarre. So, for example, I find my way around by bouncing high-frequency sound waves off nearby objects and analysing the echoes that are reflected back to me. What can it mean to experience objects as, effectively, echoes? The answer is that the problem is only apparent because we are a human pretending to be a bat. In practice, the bat has always 'seen' objects through the echoes it receives – therefore what it is aware of is *not echoes themselves, but the object revealed to it by those echoes*.

Consider the implication of this. As a human being, I see objects because light waves are focused on the retina at the back of each eye, which are then transmitted to the brain in the form of two sets of electrical impulses that the brain sorts out in order to give stereoscopic vision. But we do not see neurons firing in my brain, or electrical impulses being turned off and on, or the light waves striking the retina. Unless I want to stop and analyse the process, all I actually experience is that at which I am looking. The same must be true for the way in which the bat 'sees' things.

The conclusion Nagel came to was that no amount of information could ever tell us *what it is like to be a bat*. (Just as no amount of information about the eyeball or optic nerve is ever going to be able to tell us what it is like to see.) *'What something is like' can only be appreciated from the point of view of the experiencing subject.*

Insight

Even if I know that an experience I am having corresponds to activity in a particular part of my brain, that does not imply that the experience is identical to that activity, in the sense that to know the one is to know the other. A neurobiologist recording the brain activity would not be able to see what I see. The instruments might show that something was being experienced, but not the qualitative feel of that experience.

An appreciation of qualia tends to show the limitations of a basic materialist view. Whatever else it might be, and however it might be linked to neural activity, the actual quality and reality of an experience is not the same as a measurement of electrical activity in the brain.

So let us start with a view that is not just common sense, but also, quite simply, true – we all know what consciousness is, both as we experience it in ourselves and when we encounter it in others. We recognize it, even if we find it hard to define. Thus, for example, I know that a dog is conscious but that a stone is not. I can imagine what it might be like to be a dog, to see and respond to pleasure by wagging my tail! I have at least some idea, by analogy with my own, of what it might be like to have a dog's consciousness. On the other hand, I cannot imagine what it would be like to be a stone, to be solid and inert, without inwardness of any sort. *Consciousness is obvious; it is not the end point of a journey of discovery, but its starting point.*

There is, of course, a huge difference between human, intelligent, social behaviour and that of animals. But that difference should not lead us to assume that animals have no consciousness, or even self-awareness. Just as it would be unscientific to attempt to minimize the distinctiveness of human consciousness, so it would be equally wrong to declare, as a matter of principle, that no animal can have conscious dilemmas about action, and therefore a measure of reflective consciousness. We can observe animals working together (for example wolves or killer whales acting together to trap their prey), or a pair bonding over a number of years, but we cannot know what they feel or think. *But it would be unscientific to declare categorically that they cannot in any way feel or think, simply because we have no evidence upon which to make that claim.* That is not to suggest that we should do a Walt Disney and give animals human emotions and thoughts, simply that we should avoid the equally unwarranted assumption that animals are unconscious automata.

Example

While writing the first edition of this book I had the sad duty of burying a family pet, my daughter's dog, Sykes. Usually, on approaching the house, Sykes would come to greet me, wagging her tail in recognition. I would get licked all over. I only had to touch a lead and Sykes knew that it was time to go for a walk. She would respond to human language, sometimes turning her head to indicate that she hadn't quite understood what was said, but was interested. A familiar word would elicit an immediate response. Many photos show her curled up with my daughter, giving and receiving affection. Sykes was definitely conscious.

But this time, the familiar animal lay still on her bedding. No heartbeat, no brain activity, muscles slack; otherwise she looked fine. But, beyond the physical description, notice what is lacking – there is no response, no interaction with the world around her. The missing element is consciousness, and that would have been equally true were she in a coma rather than dead. It is impossible not to know in oneself and to recognize in others – human or animal – the essential ingredient that is consciousness.

Consciousness involves processing and responding to information that comes through the senses, but is cannot be limited to that (remember Searle's 'Chinese Room' problem – see Chapter 4). We may be conscious of having (or having had) a dream. The dream may be very significant for us, but it is not related to sense experiences. One may also be conscious of *not* receiving external stimuli. I may be conscious of feeling and seeing nothing, but nevertheless I am still conscious. Perhaps, with apologies to Descartes, one might say that 'I am conscious, therefore I am.' In other words, consciousness is what takes place where there is any sentient awareness, whether that awareness is of something internally generated, or of external stimuli. Consciousness concerns that subjective quality of experience – in other words (as defined above) its *qualia*.

But if consciousness is real, a physicalist (arguing that physical matter is the only kind of 'stuff') will expect it to be describable in physical terms. Roger Penrose controversially tried to locate consciousness at a level below that of neural firing, in a kind of quantum level of microtubes (see Chapter 9). Others (e.g. Richard Dawkins) give a reductionist account of consciousness, seeing it as a way of describing brain activity. Such reductionism – as we have seen before in terms of the general physicalist assumption of much modern philosophy of mind – is part so a wider view of the physical sciences, such that (to put it simply) biology can be reduced to chemistry, which can be then be reduced to physics. In other words, complex processes are ultimately reducible to the most basic principles of atomic physics. But none of this reveals qualia.

The alternative to such an approach is to say, along with Wittgenstein, that the self (and therefore conscious awareness) is not part of the world, but the limit of the world. Consciousness as a measurable phenomenon is not the same thing as 'what it is like' to be conscious – the former may indeed be located in neural activity and is part of the physical world, but 'what it is like' to be conscious is certainly not.

Insight

Consciousness is real – we know that, because we are conscious. But the experience of what it is like to be conscious is not discoverable as part of the physical world. That is *the* problem for the philosophy of mind, and we shall return to is again and again.

Intentionality

The psychologist Franz Brentano (1838–1917) argued that all consciousness was directed towards something. The term used for this is *intentionality*. Thus, we are not simply conscious, but also conscious 'of'. And as we consciously engage with the world, our ideas, beliefs and perceptions may be judged by their value to us and what we intend to do about them. This is a pragmatic approach, and parallels work by William James (in *Principles of Psychology*, 1890).

In modern discussion of consciousness, intentionality refers generally to the way in which our minds handle information 'about' something. I may think about an external object, or use language that involves concepts that are shared with others. The mind is not just self-referential, it does not just happen to be in a particular state; it is intentionally oriented, it is dealing 'with' something. If conscious states did not refer to anything other than themselves, they would serve no purpose, and would hold no interest for us. It is intentionality that gives the mind a task – that sets it to work on something. Thus, for example, all language is intentional.

> **Insight**
>
> We need to keep in mind just how strange this idea of intentionality is. Mental events are 'about' something other than themselves. A problem for any physicalist analysis of mind is to give an account of what this 'about' can mean – how a mental event can be itself and yet also be about something other than itself.

As we look at something, our mind gives it attention, and draws into its understanding of it a very complex set of awareness, based on our other experiences, and enhanced by our memory.

Example

The concept of 'a bowl of fruit' is actually quite a complex one. It involves the understanding that fruit is good to eat, that one might have it available at home, that it could be out on display, because it is the sort of food that one might have between meals, and so on. One might recall various artists who have painted bowls of fruit. One may remember the occasion on which one was given that particular bowl, or the moment in the shop when the fruit was bought. A simply act of looking at an object may therefore be a complex mixture of memories and experiences, which the mind holds together in that single experience.

We can describe things as conscious if they have intentionality – in other words, if they are goal-oriented and have purpose and aim in what they do. But, of course, at the simplest level, the creature concerned may not be able to reflect or comment on that purpose. Now it is far from clear how one would understand the mind of a very simple creature, but Daniel Dennett, for example, sees the 'intentional stance' – the strategy of treating behaviour as if it is governed by rational choices and goals – as a useful one. So, for example, we can say that a white blood cell has a particular purpose; it is part of the system of repair and management for the body. A white blood cell is definitely goal-oriented, and having an 'intentional stance' is the way we recognize that. But should one say that it has a mind?

Clearly, intentionality implies that the mind has conscious representations of external things. It handles informational states that represent external features of the world. But if we equate consciousness with information about external states, then there are quite a few things, like simple measuring instruments, which hold such information without being conscious. Is a barometer 'conscious' of air pressure? Does the bar scanner 'know' that goods have been passed over it? Does the gearbox 'know' that you have selected reverse rather than drive?

Dennett, in *Kinds of Minds* (1996), points out that we may perhaps perceive minds only within certain parameters of size and speed of action. If something is very large or very slow, then it is difficult to see what is happening. Plants, for example, may turn to face the sun, in this they are *sensitive* to their environment and *respond* to it. This suggests that they have what he calls an 'intentional stance'. If a person or animal swung round to get the benefit of light, or turned languidly while sunbathing, one would assume – from the fact that the person was aware of the benefits of the sun and wanted to make use of them – that the action was a clear sign of consciousness. A plant may do exactly the same thing – but may do it very slowly. Competition, rivalry, the quest for extra nutrition and sunlight: the rat-race life of plants is only displayed to us by means of speeded-up film. If they moved as quickly as animals, we might find it difficult not to think of them as conscious.

....

Insight

In considering this, we need to make a distinction between Brentano's 'intentionality' and Dennett's 'intentional stance': the former is a feature of our experience (namely that it relates to something); the latter is a way of describing activity *as if* it is happening for a purpose. In other words, Dennett is merely saying that what 'folk psychology' would describe in terms of beliefs, desires and so on, can be a useful way of describing how people behave. It is a way of predicting what we may *do*, but says nothing about what we *experience*.

A SIMPLE CONSCIOUSNESS?

If consciousness relates to informational states, the logical conclusion is that consciousness exists across a very wide range of objects, both animate and inanimate. If this idea is unacceptable, it is possible to add another qualification – namely that, for consciousness, the information must have the effect of controlling behaviour. In other words, the barometer is not conscious, since it does nothing with the information that can be read from it. But what would we then say about a barometer with a robot attached, such that, every time the pressure dropped, the robot would collect an umbrella from a cupboard and set it near the door, in case of rain? Would such a barometric robot have consciousness?

Notice that such questions bring us back to the functionalist view of mind, and to the basics of much discussion of artificial intelligence – we are back on the input (representations), processing and output (controlled behaviour) way of examining consciousness. Clearly, for something to have a mind, it must have intentionality (being sensitive and responding to its environment), but it seems to need something else as well, something that a barometer, however sensitive, simply does not have.

Crazy!

We all sense which things are conscious and which are not. We know that the mouse crouching in a corner, shuddering while the cat plays with it, is experiencing fear – although, to be fair, we cannot know exactly what it is like to be a frightened mouse. On the other hand, the elaborate piece of robotic equipment that moves about a room avoiding furniture may look conscious, and yet we automatically sense that there is no conscious life, just the obedience to programmed instructions.

> The curious thing is that we all know these things, and yet the functionalist definition of what it means to be conscious – processing information and responding to it – makes it actually very difficult not to come to the conclusion that some sort of primitive consciousness is found at almost every level of reality. Hence we end up with the crazy notion of a thermometer being conscious of temperature. But is that any more bizarre than describing as 'robotic' or 'mindless' the behaviour of people who are theoretically capable of conscious choice?

ACTIVE KNOWING...

In assessing the perspectives given by functionalism and intentionality, it is important to realize that the mind plays a very active role in cognition. We do not just experience random 'anythings', but a succession of 'somethings'. We sort them out and relate to them; we seek patterns and give significance.

In comparing different kinds of minds and the way they work, Daniel Dennett points out that animals have evolved to consume information. The further up the evolutionary path it finds itself, the more each living thing needs to take an active role is assessing and responding to its environment. In evolutionary terms, if you can move only slowly, then you need good hearing and eyesight to detect and avoid predators. Survival depends on your information gathering and processing – and hence these are developed, as the relatively blind and deaf get eaten at a younger age, and those aware of their environment survive to breed. Active knowing is the key to survival, to breeding, and hence to the development of the species. A passive mind is of little use.

Insight

Eyes do not just see, they look; ears do not just hear, they listen. If an 'intentional stance' means anything, it is the way in which a conscious being takes an active part in engaging with its environment in order to survive. Too often a discussion of consciousness has considered it in terms of our experience of data fed in through the senses. But that's to get the direction of flow wrong; conscious experience is what we get the senses to do for us.

Conscious brains?

One of the key questions is this: *How is it possible that a physical system, however complex, gives rise to the phenomenon of consciousness?* What 'extra' is there within such a system to make it possible? And, if it is not easy to see how it relates to the physical system, then how do we study it? It is, after all, a phenomenon like any other (we all know and experience it), so it ought to be susceptible to scientific explanation. We ought to be able to relate it to other features of the natural world.

We saw earlier that one of the ways cognitive science sees the mind is through what is known as the 'computationalist' approach. In effect, the mind is seen as a computer program, a set of cognitive processes in abstraction from the brain. To use the computer analogy, the brain is the hardware and the mind is the software. The problem for this approach is to see how this computation relates to the actual neural processes that are going on in the brain.

Over the second half of the 20th century, there were great advances in the understanding of what the brain actually does. Only with the advent of electron microscopes in the 1950s was it possible to see the synaptic junctions, by means of which the millions of neurons are linked with one another in sending electrical impulses of varying intensities to one another. What became clear – with the aid of fMRI (see Introduction) – was that even fairly straightforward processes could involve millions of neurons, from several different parts of the brain, but that what is experienced as a mental event involves waves of additional electrochemical activity, through specific parts of the brain, measurable in terms of the additional blood supply needed.

Another remarkable finding was that, where parts of the brain had been damaged (through an accident, for example, or a stroke) certain very specific features of thought, speech or action could be affected. By monitoring these lesions in the brain and their corresponding effects, it became possible to pick out particular sections of the brain that handle particular features of mental activity. What is more, it was found (and, of course, it can be observed in those who have suffered brain damage) that when one part of the brain is destroyed, other parts attempt to take over its function, although they generally do so far less efficiently than the damaged part, since they have previously been employed for different tasks. Clearly, the brain learns how to do things; it is not like a piece of computer hardware that knows nothing until it is programmed.

In the opening of his book *The Conscious Mind* (1996), David Chalmers makes the point that he works on the assumption that consciousness is a natural phenomenon, and that it should therefore be capable of scientific explanation, even if we cannot give one at the moment. But that, of course, does not mean that consciousness can be reduced in a materialist way. His view is that consciousness arises from the organization of what is going on in the brain, and is therefore not seen if it is simply reduced to brain activity itself.

Brain features and mind features

John Searle (in *Minds, Brains and Computers*) makes the absolutely crucial point that, although brain activity may cause mental activity, and mental operations may therefore reflect what is happening in the brain, that does not imply that the way of describing the two things will be the same, nor that one makes the other *redundant*. He gives the example of the desk at which he writes being hard, and knows that it relates to the lattice structure of the molecules of which it is made. Similarly, the wetness of water is a feature of water molecules. But that does not mean that hardness and wetness are features of something *other than* those molecules. It makes no sense at all to say that a water molecule is wet – since wetness does not show up at the molecular level. But at the same time, what is wet is nothing other than the liquid made up of molecules.

Thus, in exploring consciousness, we are dealing with features that are quite different from patters of neuron firing in the brain. But that does not mean that they are not real, and it does not mean that they do not refer to those neurons and to nothing other than them. So it is possible that a description of consciousness, and a description of the operation of the brain, may be utterly different, with neither making any sense if applied to the other, while still accepting that both kinds of language describe the same thing.

What we can say with some degree of certainty is that the neurophysiology of the brain is intimately linked with what we experience as the mental process. Brain function both *causes* and *realizes* mental states. We are not going to find some 'other' place where mind is located, but equally, it would be a reductionist folly to try to *identify* brain with mind, which is what physicalists have tended to do. Mental states – thoughts, hopes, ideas, wants, regrets – may be the experience that takes place alongside particular patterns of neurophysiological activity, but they are also related to past experiences, and to the broad area of shared consciousness that constitutes human culture.

Insight

What happens in our mind can no more be the product of a single brain than the information on the Internet can be the product of a single computer memory. When the mind thinks, it is more like 'logging on' than simply 'turning on'. Words, concepts, values, relationships and our overall situation in life – all of these things inform our mental activity. But they are not our personal property. They are certainly not contained within our skull. We are an efficient receptor of the thoughts that form the common experience of humankind. We have a past and a future. Our present brain activity is but the action we take to try to get us from the one to the other as happily as possible!

Disembodied consciousness

Before looking at whether or not consciousness can exist without a body, we need to return for a moment and consider exactly what it is we mean by consciousness. If we take it to refer to the whole range of mental activities, covering both the awareness a creature has of its environment and its response to it, then it is difficult to see how it can be disembodied, since consciousness must surely include sensation. But is sensation a mental function, or is it related to the body? We know that, while asleep, we may believe that we are receiving sensations that are not actually taking place. Does that put sensations into a separate category from other mental activities, such that deprived of sensations (which clearly must be the case if a mind is disembodied), consciousness can carry on.

One thinker who was very clear about the role of sensations was John Stuart Mill. In *The System of Logic* (1872) he categorized mental phenomena as comprising thoughts, emotions, volitions and sensations. Of the latter he said that they were:

'as truly states of Mind as the three former. It is usual, indeed, to speak of sensations as states of body, not of mind. But this is the common confusion of giving one and the same name to a phenomenon and to the proximate cause or conditions of the phenomenon. The immediate antecedent of a sensation is a state of body, but the sensation itself is a state of mind. If the word mind means anything, it means that which feels.'

Thus the external world and the bodily means of getting in touch with that world are physical, but the sensations themselves are mental. As we have seen earlier, there is always the possibility of confusion, because we speak of seeing 'a red shape', for example, and mean there exists something red in the physical world external to our body. But we have also seen that 'a red shape' only makes sense in terms of our mental process of sensation. What is 'out there' may produce light of a particular frequency, and this may be translated into nerve impulses and so on, but the actual experience of 'a red shape' is what happens when that information is received by the mind, and is recognized as a sensation.

But the crucial question for us here is this: *If sensations are mental events, and yet are caused directly by the bodily reception of stimuli from the external physical world, how it is possible for a 'mind' to exist in a disembodied state?*

One possibility here is that of someone asleep or (more significantly) in a deep coma. In these situations one may say that the mind is still active, and yet there are clearly no further sensory inputs. Hence there might be thoughts, emotions and volitions in the complete absence of sensations.

But how can we know? One possibility would be to study brain activity during sleep or of a comatose patient. But what does this show? It shows a physical, not a mental phenomenon – for brain activity, like the sensory nerves that transmit information to the brain, is clearly on the physical side of the physical/mental divide. The possibility of disembodies mental activity is only known because, on returning to consciousness, a person claims to have had that activity – in the form of dreams. There are two issues of particular interest here, the possibility of life after death, and 'out of body' experiences.

LIFE AFTER DEATH

This is a contradiction in terms, which nevertheless takes on particular significance both emotionally and for religious views of the nature of reality and human destiny.

For those taking a dualist view, mental phenomena and physical phenomena are quite different, so it might be possible to imagine the former without the latter. However, the problem with this is that there is no knowledge of mental activity other than through the mediation of physical activity. I may remember that I had a dream last night, but that act of remembering (although not *what* I remember) may be detected as brain activity. What is more, any act of reporting mental activity is physical.

Hence, even if it were possible to speculate about a dream-like state in which mental activity took place after death, one would need to ask how this would make any sense without physical activity in the brain, and how one could ever show that it had taken place. In other words, that which is not physically detectable, and cannot be reported without involving physical activity, *cannot be known*. What is more, because we have always seen mental activity joined to physical activity in the brain, we assume that it must *necessarily* be so joined.

Of course, from the religious point of view, life after death is linked to issues of great personal significance:

▶ It offers a sense of appropriate compensation, good or bad, for what a person has done or experienced during his or her life. Religious traditions generally have some element of reward or punishment beyond death for deeds done in this life, whether that is externally imposed (as in Western religions) or self-generated (as in the karma of Eastern traditions). But surely, what such beliefs are emphasizing is the transcendent nature of the mind; that a person's life has significance that goes beyond the limited fortunes of the physical body. The desire for reward or punishment is a desire that the true value of the human person should be acknowledged in a way that cannot be the case in terms of a limited physical life.

▶ It also expresses the sense that human life somehow goes 'beyond' the confines of a fragile human body – the sense that there must be something more to life than one is capable of experiencing here and now.

Neither of these constitutes *evidence* for survival of death. What they do show is the *appropriateness* of such belief for a religious person, and the reasons why he or she might hold to it in the absence of evidence.

Insight

Might fear of non-existence encourage the sense that the self continues beyond death? If so, one might reflect on Epicurus' argument that it is unreasonable to fear not-existing after death, since we cannot fear our non-existence before birth.

There are a number of logical problems that follow from the idea that minds (or selves or souls) are eternal and separable from bodies. In *Republic*, having made the point that souls are immortal, Plato has to accept that the number of souls must therefore be fixed, since the immortal cannot be produced from the mortal. The implication of this would seem to be that:

▶ *either:* every soul that has been or ever will be born, must continue to exist in an eternal realm
▶ *or:* via reincarnation, the fixed number of souls go through a succession of lives.

If either of these is the case, we can ask how the eternal self relates to the self as experienced in the physical body, which is conscious of itself through its memories and experience? Clearly, if my present self is related to my present life, we have either two selves (this one and the eternal one) or multiple selves, each relating to a particular incarnation.

While the Buddha refused to speculate about whether an enlightened person could continue after death, and his basic teaching of *anatta* suggested that there could be no fixed self, even in this life, this did not prevent *The Tibetan Book of the Dead* giving an account of souls waiting to be born and even witnessing their moment of their conception. But once you accept a dualism in which the mind arrives in this world fully formed, even if forced to forget its former incarnations, you need to be prepared to follow through its consequences – including the idea that it makes no sense to speak of selves as parents or children, since all alike are eternal, since any creature may have had a parental or filial relationship with us over the course of an infinite number of lifetimes.

Insight

The continuing popularity of belief in life after death seems to me to follow from a deep conviction that there is something about a human individual that transcends the limitations of the physical body, and a recognition that those who have died may still exert an influence over us and have some sort of 'place' within our overall view of the human world. Neither of those things is susceptible to scientific or logical investigation, but as intuitions they are none the less real for that.

NEAR-DEATH EXPERIENCES

About one-third of all those who have given accounts of having been very close to death (or even pronounced dead), but having subsequently recovered, describe what are termed 'near-death experiences'. As a phenomenon, it is neither rare, nor limited to people with any particular set of religious beliefs.

Typical of such an experience is an awareness of the self, floating above the operating table upon which one's now nearly dead body is lying, and looking down at the scene. It is generally accompanied by a sense of wellbeing, detachment from the traumas of the body, and sometimes of relief and of happy anticipation. There are frequent descriptions of moving down through a dark tunnel towards some comforting light at the end. Then there is generally a sense that one has to go back, of being physically drawn down into the body again, sometimes almost with a sense of regret.

One theory is that such experiences are brought about because the brain is starved of oxygen, and that a 'near-death experience' is actually simply the qualia associated with brain states that occur as the brain itself is 'shutting down' (to use a computer analogy). If so, it simply confirms the linking of qualia and brain states, those in the final stages of the life of a brain being reported only by those who survive such situations.

An existentialist view

Heidegger explored the nature of what he termed *Dasein*, what it is for humans 'to be'. In other words, he was looking at the nature and purpose of 'Being', seen particularly from a human standpoint. He recognized that there are many facts that determine who we are – facts about the world into which, in his terms, we are 'thrown'. We cannot escape from the 'thrownness' of our nature, any more than we can escape from the fact of death; our life in finite and lived in particular circumstances. What we can do, according to Heidegger, is make choices that reflect our personal aims in life, rather than simply conform to what others or the situation expects of us. This is what it means to live in an 'authentic' rather than an 'inauthentic' way.

Heidegger's thought is complex, and his style and language is far from easy to cope with. Nonetheless, he showed (particularly in his principal work, *Being and Time*) how the experience of human life was related to the fundamental issues of Being, and that it was lived in all three time zones, with the present always influenced by the thrownness of the past, but also the goals and aspirations that we look for in the future.

A key feature of his thought (and that of existentialism in general), for the purpose of the philosophy of mind, is the recognition that *existential questions are very different from ontological ones*. Most philosophers start by asking if the self exists, and what it can be like. Existential thinkers, however, do not ask 'if' the self exists, but rather look at *what the self is doing, and how it relates to the structures of existence*. In other words, for existentialist philosophy, the self plays a formative role, shaping itself by its decisions, always relating to other people and the rest of the world. *The self is thus a function, or process; it is not a fixed entity.* To behave in an authentic way is to express the reality of self in the light of the reality of the world; it is to affirm one's freedom to choose. To deny this is to retreat back into the idea that everything is determined by outside influences (the 'they' for Heidegger) and the thrownness of our origins, whereas the true vocation of humanity is to live in a way that is authentic and free from external constraints, following our goals by making concrete decisions about how we are to live.

Jean-Paul Sartre (1905–80) argued that consciousness was always consciousness 'of' something, and was therefore not an entity in itself. Consciousness is related to everything that is not itself. In this sense, consciousness is a 'total emptiness'.

Insight

If we try to look at our own consciousness, we see it as a 'thing', but in so doing it becomes part of the world of which we are conscious. In other words, we are trying to make an object out of subjectivity, which is impossible. *Consciousness is like an eye that sees everything except itself*; therefore Sartre can describe consciousness as a 'non-substantial absolute'.

In many ways, this is like Wittgenstein's saying that the self is not *part* of the world, but rather the *boundary* of the world.

There is another important element to the existentialist approach. Sartre makes the distinction between 'being in itself' and 'being for itself'. The latter is the personal subject, aware of itself in its relationships with the external world. 'Being in itself', by contrast, is being insofar as it is a fixed 'object', something that just 'is' but which does not ask existential questions.

To see the self as 'being in itself' is to limit it, to see it simply in terms of how it responds to external influences, to reduce it to a thing that can be observed and shaped. It is rather like Heidegger's 'inauthentic' self that only responds to the bidding of external forces. By contrast, 'being for itself' is an *active agent*, defining and shaping itself through choices made as a result of its contact with the world.

Clearly, consciousness is to do with 'being for itself'; but the problem of looking at consciousness is that there is a tendency to objectivize it, to show where it 'fits in' – in other words, to make it 'being in itself'. Analysed in this way, it is no surprise that consciousness vanished.

In other words, the self is that which gives meaning and significance to life, choosing the future and responding to influences from the past. It can do so precisely to the extent that it does not allow itself to be objectivized, or put within a causal structure that denies its very essence.

The bicameral mind

One of the most fascinating books on the development of consciousness, primarily in the sense of self-awareness, is *The Origin of Consciousness in the Breakdown of the Bicameral Mind* by Julian Jaynes (Houghton Mifflin, 1977; Penguin, 1990). It is relevant here because it argues that there was a time (around 3,000 years ago) when people started to become aware of themselves in a new way, entering into dialogues with themselves as they decided what they should do. Prior to that there was a sense of external forces speaking directly and controlling human activity.

Quite apart from the fascinating questions this raises for the philosophy of mind, it is also of interest for those considering the phenomenon of religion, for Jaynes' theory would suggest that present belief in God or the gods is a residual feature of that more primitive state of human consciousness when humans were far more aware than now of apparently 'external' voices commanding their attention.

10 THINGS TO KEEP IN MIND

1 'Qualia' are the phenomenal qualities of experience – colours, sounds and so on.

2 The 'hard' problem is knowing how brain processes can generate the experience of qualia, and thus how to find a place for consciousness within the natural world.

3 Intentionality refers to the fact that our mental experiences are always 'of' something other than themselves.

4 Brain scans show neural activity, but cannot themselves show qualia.

5 Consciousness is recognized through the engagement of an individual being with its environment.

6 Consciousness relates to language and to society; it is not simply the product of a physical individual.

7 Having no body with which to communicate, a disembodied consciousness, even if logically possible, would be unknowable.

8 Life after death does not make sense logically or scientifically but reflects personal convictions about the nature of the self.

9 For Heidegger, the self is always related to both past and future.

10 Existentialists see the self as an active, subjective agent.

6

Mind and the theory of knowledge

In this chapter you will:
- *examine theories about how we gain knowledge*
- *consider whether all our knowledge comes from experience*
- *explore the way we interpret our experience.*

The theory of knowledge (*epistemology*) has always been a crucial feature of philosophy because, unless we know *how* we know what we know, we have no means of deciding whether any claim to knowledge is true or false. In this chapter we shall examine some theories about how we gain knowledge in the light of our consideration of the nature of mind.

To know is to remember

Plato held that one could have opinions about particular objects presented to the senses, but that certain knowledge was limited to the ideal realm of the 'Forms' – universals of which those particular things were examples. But, clearly, the Forms could not be seen directly. Plato therefore believed that all true knowledge was a matter of remembering; that an awareness of the Forms is already innate in us prior to birth, and guides us to have our opinions about the particular things we see.

Now, we need not be concerned here about Plato's theory of knowledge itself, but it does have crucial implications for his view of the mind. If Plato is correct, then the mind has within itself a set of principles and general ideas that are there *before* any experience.

We recognize things in the world as being, for example, a particular breed of dog or species of tree, because we already have some general knowledge of what we mean by 'dog' or 'tree'. The mind is therefore not the product of cumulative experience, built up by responding to the world, but comes to us, as it were, ready formed with a stock of eternal truths.

One standard criticism of Plato's theory runs like this:

- ▶ I know that this thing I see before me is a man.
- ▶ I do so because I already have a general concept 'man'.
- ▶ But how do I know that this individual is in fact a particular example of the general concept 'man', unless there is a 'third man' to whom they can both be related?
- ▶ In other words, I can never be sure that this particular resembles the general 'Form' because, in order to prove that, I would need to show that the Form and the individual had a common set of characteristics – and that set of characteristics would amount to another 'idea' or 'Form', and so on ad infinitum.

Plato believed that the self or soul was immortal and had lived many times before. Hence, he believed that knowledge was essentially a matter of recollection. This is discussed in his dialogue *Meno*, where he asks a servant boy a series of mathematical questions, and observes how he works out the answers. He concludes that the boy could not have been taught those answers in this life; therefore he must have recalled them from past lives.

Few today might use the way we know things as an argument for existence pre-birth, as Plato did, but the issue of whether we have innate ideas is still very relevant. Clearly, we see things 'as', rather than just registering sense impressions. But such 'seeing as' implies that we have concepts and general principles by which we make sense of particular sensations. How have we acquired those concepts? Are our brains already 'hard-wired' for them? Are we programmed with them, just as Chomsky suggested that we were born with a natural facility to recognize and learn a language? Are they structural features of the brain? How can you have concepts without experiences: in other words, what could the general concept 'tree' mean for someone who had never seen a particular tree?

Mind and certainty

How can we be certain about those things we experience? There are two approaches to answering this question:

1 We can ask how it is possible to know that the perceptions we have actually resemble objects that are external to us. The philosopher and essayist Michel de Montaigne (1533–92) argued that, if one had never seen Socrates, one could not claim that a portrait of the philosopher was a good likeness. If we cannot know things except through our perceptions, how can we ever know whether or not those perceptions are accurate? That, of course, was the question posed by Plato. The implication of this question, for some thinkers, is that we must have some innate knowledge prior to experience if we are to be certain of anything.

2 However, John Locke argued that there is a basic resemblance between our perceptions and the external world. He had to take this view because he also believed that the mind started off as a blank sheet of paper and only built up knowledge through experience. Locke saw the mind as fundamentally a storing and sorting facility – making sense of experiences. While he recognized that some aspects of experience (the secondary qualities of colour, taste, etc.) were related to our sense organs, the primary qualities of extension and number were external to us, and not mind-dependent. Thus, even if we cannot specify *how* our experience relates to the external world, we have to assume it does – and that, of course, fits with the common-sense view of what our senses are about, namely that they give us information, even if they shape it in the process of doing do.

DESCARTES' DILEMMA

Of what, then, can we be certain? This was the key question asked by Descartes – and his view of the separation of mind that body that came from it has been, as we have already seen, hugely influential. Descartes was much influenced by the general scepticism of his day. He recognized the force of Montaigne's argument that one could not know whether perceptions gave a true picture of reality. He knew that in dreams he could experience what he believed to the real at the time, only to find on awakening that it had been no more than a dream. Asking the fundamental question 'By what criterion can you show that this is true?' he realized that certainty could only be given if the basis on which one made that judgement was certain. But what if that basis were also open to question? You can't prove that something is true unless you have a criterion of which you are certain, but you can't prove *that*, without something else being shown to be certain, and so on. In the end, there seemed no fixed point of certainty – a sceptical view that was widespread in Descartes' day.

Against Plato's innate knowledge on the one hand, and Locke's knowledge through senses on the other, Descartes recognized the force of such scepticism. He therefore sought that elusive point of certainty, without which all claims would remain vulnerable to the sceptic's challenge.

The vehicle he uses to express this (see *Meditation II*) is a powerful and malicious genius which is determined to deceive him. Faced with such a deceiver, of what can he be certain? Of his body? Of his movements? He recognizes that bodily movements can be experienced in dreams, when they are clearly not real, so he cannot be sure of any of them, and therefore cannot trust his sensations. What then of thought, can he doubt that he is a thinking being? And, of course, unable to doubt that one thing (since the act of doubting was in itself an intellectual act), he arrived at 'I think therefore I am.'

Hence his dualism – and all that has followed from it – is rooted in his theory of knowledge. It appeared to him to be the only means of countering the force of sceptical doubt. But the price of that certainty is that the mind (and self) is limited to its thinking function, and is effectively removed from the physical.

The problem is that we cannot separate our understanding of what the mind is from the *process* by which we gain knowledge, or justify our claims to knowledge. Do we pre-date our experiences, or are we a product of them? Is there some separate, eternal 'me' that has a reality independent of the circumstances in which I find myself, or am I inevitably moulded and shaped by everything that happens, my initially blank mind learning and developing as it passes through life?

Some implications of this

Although we'll return to these questions again later, notice their ethical and political implications. If you are entirely moulded by your environment, then it (rather than you) is responsible for your actions. The poor rat in the Skinner box has been programmed to keep touching its lever in the hope of reward. If all we learn comes through our experience, are we any more independent of our circumstances than that rat?

By the same token, is it every possible to encounter someone whose mind touches on universal themes, rising above circumstances, background or conditioning, and presenting ideas or values that cannot be accounted for sociologically?

How we treat people will be coloured by the conclusions we reach on these questions. Do I wish to be seen by you as someone who is simply a product of a certain upbringing and environment? Can my mind have ideas that are not simply a product of circumstances?

In Chapter 2 we outlined Berkeley's reasons for saying that all we can know are our sense perceptions and that, although we assume that they correspond to an external world, nevertheless we have no direct knowledge of such a world, only of our perception of it.

Knowledge, therefore, for Berkeley, is limited to thinking about sense perception and the concepts by which we make sense of it. We cannot somehow get outside, or around, our perceptual apparatus to get an alternative view of the world, by which we can then assess its reliability. The object and our sensation of it are the same thing; our world is a world of ideas. But if sensations are all we know, it is difficult to see how we can be sure of anything. But surely I have to trust that the world is as I experience it. I can't prove it, because I can't get outside my experience, but without some basic assumption that it is so, life would become impossible.

Berkeley, of course, brings God into the equation, as guarantor of continuity. The world has continued to exist even when nobody is there to perceive it because it is always perceived by God.

Insight

Nevertheless, it is difficult not to see Berkeley as effectively caught in the modern dilemma about whether the light has actually gone out once the fridge door is closed!

We see it our way

What does it mean to perceive something? I see a creature in front of me and know that it is a cat – no problem. But, actually, in order to see this thing as a cat there are a number of mental operations to be performed. To start with, size. The cat may be near or far, but – by the way in which my eyes focus and in comparison with other things of which I already know the size – I calculate the size of the cat. But that is not simply something that comes with the impact of light rays on the retina of my eyes; it is a mental operation.

But what makes it a 'cat'? Not its colour – for there are cats of many different colours. What about having four legs and a tail? Fine, but I will have sympathy for the three-legged cat, and have no reason for claiming that a Manx cat is not feline simply because it lacks a tail. The process of seeing a cat therefore involves a number of straight computational processes, but more particularly an appreciation of which features are *essential* for it to be called a 'cat' and which are *incidental*. My perceiving of a cat is therefore related to my education; I have been told (with many examples) that certain things are to be called 'cats', and so that it how I now categorize them.

Cats, of course, are an obvious example. Take a more subtle form of the same dilemma. You taste the wine from a bottle whose label has been inconveniently covered. If you are a connoisseur of wines, you may immediately guess where it is from, its vintage, perhaps the particular vineyard. It is not that the novice has a different experience, but that – without training and the development of a suitable palate – wines cannot be experienced with such subtlety.

No ordinary brandy

On a visit to Cognac, I was able to look through the glass panels of the door into the tasting room. There the most experienced tasters, with racks of eaux-de-vie in front of them, work to achieve exactly the right blend of flavours to produce their particular style of brandy. To learn exactly how to identify that taste takes many years. The nose of the head taster is a valuable possession, and the next generation of nose is already in training to take over on the retirement of the present one!

Don't try telling anyone in that room that everyone has the same sensation when tasting brandy. They have trained for years to develop the art of taste!

▶ What do we learn from this? That the subtlety and complexity of an experience is related to the training and abilities of the person who does the experiencing.
▶ If, by scanning, it can be shown that the relevant neural pathways of the experienced tasters have been rendered more efficient by their training, it shows that the mind (including the social phenomenon of blending alcoholic beverages) can shape the operations of the brain.

We see it 'our' way; and that 'our' includes our interests, experiences and social setting. To the reductionist who might suggest that the ability to taste subtle differences is simply a phenomenon of the brain, we can ask how it is that the brain has developed that ability. It is certainly not the product of natural selection, for there is no evidence that experienced tasters of eaux-de-vie outlive or outbreed those of humbler palates. Rather, the brain has responded to the intentions of the ambitious and well-practised taster.

There is a general issue in the philosophy of mind about whether our ideas are internal, or whether they only make sense in the context of our external environment. The words I use only makes sense because of the language I share with other people. Equally, an act of perception depends on shared experience – I experience things and describe them in ways that are socially conditioned. To say 'this scene is beautiful' does not simply articulate a feeling of pleasure, but describes it using a term (and thus presupposing a whole discussion and range of experiences) that are conjured up by the word 'beautiful'.

In other words, beauty is not simply in the eye (and mind) of the beholder; it is a shared concept that the beholder uses in order to express and share his or her views. Both the perception (heightened if we are trained to appreciate the subtleties of it) and the expression are social acts.

Innateness

Immanuel Kant (1724–1804) argued that the mind imposes categories (space, time and causality) upon experience, and therefore that is has an active rather than passive role. The implication of this is that we are predisposed to think that everything will have a cause, and that we have no option but to see everything falling within an overall framework of space and time.

But why do we appear to have these innate ideas or structures? Why does our mind have to work in that way? We have already seen that Plato considered knowledge to be a matter of recollection from a life in the world of the Forms from before our birth. In other words, certain ideas and abilities are innate.

Descartes took a similar view (as explained in his *Optics*), namely that, when the senses transmit information to the mind, that information is quite different from the experience that arises because of it. It becomes, as it were, the occasion for the mind to form its ideas, which is an innate faculty it has. And, of course, the reason Descartes holds this is that, according to his mechanics, the senses can only communicate through the physical movement of bodies – and he has no way of translating such physical movement into the objects of thought. Hence, the conceptions that form our basic awareness, as well as our more formal ideas, must be innate. They may be *triggered* by the senses, but cannot be created by them.

Locke pointed out that the reason people argued for innate ideas was that there were certain things that were universally agreed, and that such agreement suggested that everyone was born with them. He suggested that you should not use universal agreement as an argument for innateness unless you could show that there was no other reason why all should not agree. He points out that logical statements (e.g. something cannot both be and not be) may appear to be universal, but that in fact most people in the world have never thought about the matter at all, so they cannot be said to have assented to it. He also points out that children and idiots have no idea of what such things might mean – whereas, if such logical claims were indeed innate, then they would immediately recognize them to be true. Indeed, he sees the function of reason as the discovery of things not yet known on the basis of what is already known, but how can that be so if all knowledge is innate?

His famous conclusion is that there are no innate ideas, but that the mind is initially a tabula rasa – a blank sheet – awaiting information from the senses. This is the general position taken by empiricists, who hold that all knowledge comes through sense experience.

As mentioned above (in Chapter 3) in connection with Chomsky's argument for the innate ability to develop language, there needs to be a distinction made between *innate capabilities* and *innate knowledge*. Both empiricist and rationalists might hold that people can have innate capabilities, in other words that they have skills that cannot be accounted for in terms of that individual's experience. Those capabilities might, for example, by given by virtue of the way in which the species has evolved, and in this sense the individual benefits from millennia of experience. What the empiricist cannot accept, however, is the idea of any innate content of knowledge.

The phenomenological fallacy

In an important article in the *British Journal of Psychology*, published in 1956, the philosopher U.T. Place asked 'Is Consciousness a Brain Process?' He set out his task thus:

> *'It is argued that the problem of providing a physiological explanation of introspective observations is made to seem more difficult that it really is by the "phenomenological fallacy", the mistaken idea that descriptions of the appearance of things are descriptions of the actual state of affairs in a mysterious internal environment.'*

Quoted in R. Cummins and D.D. Cummins (eds), *Minds, Brains and Computers*, p. 361

Before setting out the fallacy, he makes two important points:

1 That we have cognitive concepts (knowing, believing, etc.) and volitional concepts (wanting, intending, etc.) and that, to express consciousness, we use what amounts to an 'inner process' story. But statements about this story cannot be the same as statements about brain processes.

2 That 'is' can be used in two ways – for definition and for composition. (For example: 'His home is a caravan' – this does not mean that the term 'home' is identical to, or explained by, the term 'caravan'; it simply means that he uses a caravan as his home.)

Taking these things into account, it is clear that one can give two very different accounts of the same thing, both of which are equally valid. Thus, to use one of his examples, a cloud is also a mass of fine water droplets in suspension. From the outside we see a cloud; from within it we see this fog of water droplets – different descriptions, different perspectives, but the same reality.

Now, the 'phenomenological fallacy' is to suppose that, when I see a red flower, there is some image of a red flower in my brain – rather as though the inside of my head formed a miniature television set – and that, therefore, there are two things happening at once, a pattern of neurons firing off, and (at the same time) a red image.

When you 'see' something, the sensations are relayed to your brain and interpreted there. Your consciousness is that process. To an external observer, it takes the form of eyeball, lens, retina, optic nerve and the stimulation of those sections of the brain responsible for sight. *You* can't see it that way, of course, because you are the one who is doing the seeing!

Comment

Although it sounds crazy, the experience of thinking and imagining is a bit like watching an internal television, so it is understandable that we might assume that that our thoughts and sensations are going on somewhere inside our heads, even if they bear no resemblance to the grey matter with which our skulls are filled.

Stand back from the situation for a moment, and consider exactly what it is to see a red flower. The sensory data, in the form of light of a certain wavelength reflected off the flower, enters my eye and falls on the retina. It is turned into electrical impulses that convey the information to my brain. The actual seeing of the red flower (and recognizing it as a 'red flower', since I have had similar experiences in the past that have been related to the use of those two descriptive words) corresponds to neurons firing in my brain.

But there cannot be *two* flowers – one out there and the other inside my head. There is only one flower, and recognizing it is as such is a function that involves my eyes, optic nerve and brain.

In the crude version of the fallacy – and an impression often given by a first reading of Locke and other empiricists – is that a human being is rather like a robot with television cameras and other sensors on the outside, relaying messages to another little person (myself) on the inside.

But that can't work, because the little internal 'me' would then also be gathering data, just like the external robot, and I would then require an even smaller 'real me' on the inside to unscramble and appreciate it. And so on ad infinitum!

Place's conclusion was:

> *'Once we rid ourselves of the phenomenological fallacy we realise that the problem of explaining introspective observations in terms of brain processes is far from insuperable. We realise that there is nothing that the introspecting subject says about his conscious experience which is inconsistent with anything the physiologist might want to say about the brain processes which cause him to describe the environment and his consciousness of the environment in the way that he does.'*

Insight

It is difficult to overestimate the importance of recognizing this fallacy. When we 'see' something, we do not see it in our brain, but in the external world. *We do not describe our consciousness; we describe the things of which we are conscious.*

The brain is not some library or exhibition, where books or pictures are lined up ready for us to compare with external reality. Rather, it is an incredibly complex organ for recording, analysing, remembering and responding to the great variety of sensations that come its way in the form of electrochemical impulses.

There is only one world, and you are a conscious part of it for as long as your brain is actively processing your encounter with your environment, or remembering previous encounters.

Pragmatism and Gestalt

What is knowledge for? Why do we acquire it? These are relevant questions for the theory of knowledge, because if you know what it is for you can understand why it is acquired in the way that it is. Pragmatists – such as John Dewey (1859–1952) – argued that you should not separate the *content* of thought from its *function*. People learn things because they need to know them. Hence it is possible to look at the mind in terms of the way it enables people to engage with and respond to the challenges they face.

This led Dewey to develop fundamental views on the nature of education, set out in his *The School and Society* (1899). Children learn best, he argued, by being presented with challenges and questions, rather than be forced to learn information that had no immediate relevance to them.

Pragmatism recognizes that the mind is 'for' something. It is not occult and mysterious, but extremely useful. Its operations are not in some unobservable world, but are seen in the problem-solving process.

Squirrels can learn to negotiate various obstacles in order to get at food. Whatever thought is required to enable the squirrel to achieve this is prompted by the need to be where that food it. Similarly, the tit that learns to peck away at a milk bottle top in order to get a drink is not simply responding to an abstract stimulus, but it performing an operation that has been learned in order to achieve an end result. Animal behaviour is pragmatic – it has an end in view – and so does the human process of acquiring knowledge.

It is worthwhile keeping the pragmatic approach in mind when thinking about the relationship between brain activity and consciousness. It is sometimes argued that consciousness is just a by-product of brain activity (essentially the epiphenomenalist approach – see Chapter 2), but that leaves out of account the question of why the brain is active and why consciousness developed in the first place. Taking a simple functionalist account, the brain would not know to instruct the body to raise an arm in self-protection if it were not for the sensory awareness of being about to be hit, and a conscious desire to avoid injury. These (however you choose to describe them) are features of the mind and consciousness, and without them the brain would have no reason to send out the signals to raise the arm.

Insight

Don't just think about *how* activity is produced; think about *why* it is produced. The answer to that, as evolutionary thinking suggests, is the key to understanding why the human body, brain and mind has developed as it has. To return to an analogy used earlier – if you want to understand a car journey, look at the reason for travelling; don't try taking the car engine apart!

Gestalt was a reaction against the early structuralist and behaviourist approaches to psychology (see Chapter 3). It argued that it is a fundamental mistake to assume that the mind understands things by analysing them into their constituent parts. Rather, the mind puts together various elements of experience in order to build up an overall picture, a whole within which the parts can make sense. In doing this, it is active in interpreting and comparing experiences; it is not merely responding to individual stimuli. The mind thinks through possibilities related to the *whole* of our world; that is the context in which it works.

Taken together, pragmatism and Gestalt theory give a very different impression of what the mind actually does, compared with the behaviourist approach. *It is active, problem solving and concerned to make sense of individual sensations in terms of the whole of experience.*

Insight

Watch a baby immediately after birth as it seeks out a nipple in order to feed. Its mind is already playing an active role in searching for nourishment. The cry of a hungry baby is not simply a response to discomfort; it is a demand to be fed! Its learning process monitors such demands and whether they work or not, and within a very few years it will be devising complex strategies for getting what it wants. The mind might start as a tabula rasa in terms of content, but it also starts with an active potential to engage with its world.

10 THINGS TO KEEP IN MIND

1 Plato thought that we had knowledge of the Forms before birth.

2 By contrast, Locke saw the mind as a tabula rasa prior to experience

3 Descartes' quest was for a point of certainty in the face of sceptical doubt.

4 If existence depends of perception, Berkeley required God to give continuity to the unperceived.

5 We perceive everything 'as' and relate it to known concepts.

6 The senses can be trained; therefore neural pathways can be influenced by the mind.

7 There is a difference between having innate knowledge and having innate capabilities.

8 The phenomenological fallacy wrongly locates the phenomena of experience within the head.

9 Knowledge is gained for a purpose and can be assessed pragmatically.

10 The mind actively seeks knowledge; it is not simply a passive recipient of sensations.

7

Personal identity and memory

In this chapter you will:
- *explore the contribution of memory and society to personal identity*
- *examine the phenomenon of worrying*
- *consider why we construct personal maps.*

Most of the issues in the philosophy of mind are concerned with, or imply, views on the nature of personal identity. The whole issue of artificial intelligence, for example, raises the question of whether a computer can be regarded as a person with an individual identity. So in this chapter we shall look at some attempts to state clearly what is meant by being a 'person', and also at some of the key issues, like memory and the phenomenon of worrying, which imply a clear sense of the being an individual with a definite identity.

Identity and individuality

Ordinarily, the words 'identity' and 'individuality' are used for much the same thing – what makes a person in some way special; their character and particular appearance. In a philosophical context, however, we may need to distinguish them.

Ever since the time of Plato, thinkers have discussed how particular things relate to their 'Form' or the general description of their kind or species. In other words, how do I know that this particular thing in front of me is a tree? How does its *individuality* (being a particular size, shape and colour) relate to the general description 'tree'? So 'individuality' is the term most appropriately used for that which distinguishes between examples of a particular kind or species. We are all 'people' but we are also all individuals. By contrast, a paperclip is unlikely to have individuality. It will be exactly the same as all the others in the box, unless I have already used it and bent it out of shape, or in some other way distinguished it from the others.

On the other hand, people change a great deal over time. The baby, adult and old person in a range of photographs may look quite different, but we are told that they are one and the same person. Personal identity therefore refers to that which remains constant for an individual, and which may therefore be used to distinguish him or her from others, who may – at this moment – share the same characteristics. Soldiers wear uniforms in order to suppress their individuality, but may nevertheless carry an identity card.

In the quest for personal identity, there are various aspects that can be examined, for example:

- ▶ bodily continuity
- ▶ continuity of character
- ▶ memory.

Thus, to the question 'Are you the same person who…?', one could argue first of all that you have to be the same person if there is bodily continuity. Indeed, this is the usual way of recognizing someone, although it is difficult if a long time has passed since last we saw him or her. But just how much change can happen to a body for this identity to remain? The old man and the baby are physically totally different, but yet can claim to be the same person. Mentally, the person with advanced Alzheimer's disease is hardly the bright young student of years before. Names give continuity, as does genetic code – but names can be changed, and genetic code is not visible; for practical purposes; therefore, we tend to supplement the basic continuity of the body, with other indications of identity. We may look for continuity in terms of that person's character and behaviour patterns. I could say 'she's not the same person I knew at college' without trying to deny bodily continuity.

But, most importantly, a person asserts who they are, and shows that they are the same person encountered earlier, by recalling events in the past. Not only do I have a sense of my own identity through my memories, but I can convey that sense of identity to others by telling my personal story, or be recalling shared moments. If adults meet for the first time since childhood, they can restore the bond of friendship, by remembering shared childhood experiences – the person encountered in the present may look and sound totally different, but memory immediately established a deep connection.

But can a person's identity always be established, and does it have a fundamental unity? Clearly, when it comes to the body, it is possible to lose a limb without thereby losing one's identity. The body is clearly divisible and some parts are going to be more crucial to personal identity than others – the successful transplant of another head would cause more problems than a transplanted liver, for example.

However, when it comes to the mind, traditional Cartesian dualism has argued that the mind is not physical and is therefore unextended. The implication of this is that it cannot be divided, since you can only divide that which occupies space. For Descartes, therefore, there is a single self with privileged access to its own mind.

From a materialist/physicalist point of view, however, it should be possible to divide off aspects of personal identity, simply because they inhere in, or are ways of describing, something physical, and the physical world is always divisible. In other words:

▶ from a **dualist** point of view, there is always going to be, at the core of personality and consciousness, a single mind – the 'real' me
▶ from a **materialist** point of view, there is always the possibility that what I conventionally call myself is a bundle of various mental aspects, a bundle whose integrity is not assured, and which might change with time.

This 'bundle' view – associated particularly with Hume and with the Buddha – may suggest a lack of personal coherence, offering no single thing that is the self. However, notice what is implied by the word 'bundle'; it is a collective term and assumes a boundary. The fact that we are a bundle makes a collection out of what might otherwise be a random assortment of sensations, experiences and memories.

We can also take genetic identity into account. Genes determine the sort of physical body that is being developed from the fertilized egg, and with that development comes the learning process by which experiences are processed and mental skills and language developed. In other words, from the moment of conception there has been a unique development, embodying many physical, mental and dispositional changes. Even if all the separate components of that person appear to change, the underlying process by which the complex entity of formed and developed gives it an identity.

Heraclitus said that one could not step into the same river twice, in the sense that the water of that river was constantly changing. However, that did not require that rivers should not be given a name, nor that one should be surprised to find it still flowing the next day. The river is a changing phenomenon, in the sense that its material is constantly flowing, but its formal identity remains.

Hence we could consider the individual, like the river, to be a bundle of ever-changing strands – physical, mental, emotional and social. In an absolute (or certainly a material) sense there is no overall continuity that can be specified in terms of a fixed quality or material, but, conventionally, we need some way of describing an entity that exists in a process of change.

Example

A school remains a school even though its pupils change year by year, its members of staff arrive and leave, and its buildings are occasionally replaced; it can even be relocated elsewhere. The school cannot therefore be defined by any physical continuity. Its identity is an ever-changing bundle of pupils, staff, buildings and so on. But it has an identity nonetheless. Might we consider the human being in much the same way, as a defined but changing bundle?

Social and role identity

In looking at social roles, we need to keep in mind, once again, the distinction between identity and individuality. Individuality is easily accounted for in terms of the theoretically infinite number of circumstances that have to come together in order to produce you as an individual. Working back from the present moment, there are the endless chances in life that have given you your experiences and shaped your views.

Further back still, there is the most decisive moment for establishing your individuality – the moment of your conception. But that only took place because of a number of variables in terms of your parents meeting one another and all that followed from it, and their parents before them, and so on. (This was explored by Heidegger, in his idea of the 'thrownness' of human life – we are pitched into life with a given set of facts over which we have no control, and which therefore start to define who we are – see Chapter 5.)

Insight

Ultimately, the whole universe has to have been exactly as it is, for you to have been produced exactly as you are. Any changes anywhere in the system, and everything else changes at the same time. The complexity of the self is a reflection of the interlocking complexity of its natural and social environment.

Your individuality is therefore established by the countless variables that affect every action in life. But society would be chaotic if individuals did not in some way mask out or limit the expression of their individuality and the freedom of experiencing endless possibilities is too much for people to cope with. We therefore retreat behind masks of convention, in order to get on with the business of living and dealing with others. Hence, we accept identities established by our roles within our various circles of influence – for example:

▶ through close relationships – as a son or daughter of, father or mother of, brother or sister, and so on
▶ as a member of a particular interest group or group of friends
▶ through a work environment – as a student in a particular faculty, or as a manager or executive in a business, as a worker or member of a union

- as one who holds certain views or ideas, perhaps expressed as a political or religious allegiance
- in terms of origins – as coming from a particular country, or having a rural or urban upbringing
- as a citizen of a country or member of a race.

Each of these identities is useful to the extent that it defines you over against those who do not belong to the same group. Thus there would be no point in claiming to be an Earthling while on planet Earth, whereas such an identity would take on meaning if your spaceship were on a voyage to a distant galaxy!

At different times, and for different purposes, each of these will become more or less relevant. Relationships establish a sense of identity, and the closer the relationship, the more significant will be its influence. But notice what is happening as we consider social relationships. We are not trying to analyse the self, breaking it down to establish what gives it continuity and therefore identity. Rather we are considering the *whole* self as it relates to features of its environment, and as it makes choices against its background.

Where are you?

Where is a friendship located? Is it in your head? Surely it cannot be, since it is a shared reality. Where is a conversation? Where is the sense of national identity, or the local community? Where is your family actually located?

Physical location is relatively unimportant in establishing social identity. Rather like a website that conveys information to anyone who accesses it, the key thing is what it says, not the particular server on which it is lodged.

It is important to keep this in mind, since it is always tempting to locate the self in the head, rather than seeing it as a social phenomenon.

Social identity is therefore a matter of *synthesis*, not of *analysis*. You are the sum total of the person who acts, not some inner or 'real' part that can be abstracted from the rest of your body or mind, and you act as a 'person' within the various contexts of your life, physical, mental and social.

A philosopher who emphasized the priority of 'persons' (and who started doing so in the days before the rise of cognitive science, when the issue of identity was still being considered largely from a linguistic perspective, following the influence of Ryle) was P.F. Strawson (1919–2006), a British philosopher known particular for his work on the nature of identity. In 'Persons', an article published in 1958, and his book *Individuals* (1959), he argued that the concept of 'person' was such that both physical characteristics and states of consciousness could be ascribed to it. In other words, one does not have to start with minds and bodies and then see if they can be put together to form persons; rather one starts with 'persons' and any subsequent analysis is optional.

People exist in a social context. Their identity is not established by analysis of attributes, nor can it be revealed in a brain scan, but by examining how they relate to others, contribute to friendships, family groups, nations and so on. *The concept of 'person' and personal identity emerges only in this holistic context.*

Insight

However, we also need to be aware of the danger that we will identify totally with one or more of the social roles that we adopt. Heidegger, while accepting that we are always tempted to hide behind a social mask, thereby exposed the artificiality of doing so, and of the possibility of authentic experience. You are more than any one of your social roles, but are you more than the sum total of them? That is the crucial question.

There is also a far broader context here for understanding our identity. Who we are is largely influenced by both language and culture. Indeed, it is one of the tragedies of the domination of one race or nation by another that it deprives the dominated of any real sense of personal and social identity. In order to be ourselves, we need to tell a story about who we are. This is found both in terms of religious narratives and political ones. Our identity is reaffirmed by our story, by an account of our family, historical and cultural roots. This is related, of course, to what Daniel Dennett describes in terms of a narrative 'centre of gravity', in *Consciousness Explained*. We spin out our stories, as a spider spins a web, but as the stories are repeated, they spin us, in the sense that they inform our conscious selfhood.

Memory

As we have already seen, memory is an important factor in establishing identity. You are what you are because you have learned from the past, your values and attitudes are shaped by your experience – and that depends on memory. A person without a memory might still have a whole variety of skills, but would otherwise be quite lost. Without memory there is no recognition, and without recognition it is difficult to respond to whatever is presented to the senses.

Memory is private. David Hume saw memory in terms of a sequence of private images running through his head. If I say I remember something, it is difficult for someone else to contradict me, unless there is evidence that I physically could not have been where I claim to remember having been. Police, in interviewing a suspect, will be challenging his or her claimed memory on exactly those grounds.

There is also a difference between remembering skills (how to walk), logical or mathematical principles ($2 \times 2 = 4$), and remembering particular events. Someone suffering from amnesia may retain such skills, while being unable to recall events. Skills are generally remembered instantly – I do not have to think how to walk; I just do it. Neuroscience has also shown us that the exercise of a skill 'trains' the brain to do it more efficiently. Thus, for example, a person who practises playing a musical instrument may, by doing so, facilitate the operation of those neural pathways that operate the finger muscles, thereby giving added dexterity. In effect, the brain fine-tunes itself to fit in with our particular needs and circumstances. This does not necessarily imply that every act is laid down in the memory in a way that can be recalled, but that we have an entirely natural and unconscious ability to develop and learn from the past.

However, responding to the question 'Where were you at the time the crime was committed?' may require considerable time and effort, and involves quite a different aspect of memory, often aided by putting together other remembered details and making connections. But the question is asked simply because our memories are private, and we alone are able to access them. However, the fact that we have privileged access to our own memories does not mean that we are infallible. Two people may give very different accounts of a meeting, since memories are selective, including those things that are deemed significant, and ignoring those that are not.

Insight

We need to recognize that we become the person we are because of both kinds of mental activity. Unconsciously, the activities we engage in will tune our brains to be able to do them more effectively, giving us a range of skills, but we are also able consciously to access memories of particular events, and these shape our present interpretation of life, because they give us a history and experience of things loved or hated that shape our views and choices.

MEMORY AND THERAPY

As we go through life, our thoughts, emotions and attitudes are shaped by our experiences. Some of the influences are conscious; others (particularly from the earliest stages of life) are unconscious. In either case, what appears to be happening is that experience leads to patterning. An experience (whether pleasant or painful) leads to the anticipation of what will happen to us when we encounter something similar in the future. Hence, we have a pattern by which to assess the present and anticipate the future. If a particular aspect of life has brought us trauma in the past, we will (consciously or unconsciously) carry that pattern of expectation with us.

It is the ability to remember the past that makes therapy effective in changing attitudes and emotions in the present. If it were not for memory, we would not be able to learn, or adapt our behaviour in line with experience. Clearly, this is most clearly illustrated in the process of counselling or psychotherapy. It is in exploring the past that we find the roots of our present emotional states.

The past cannot be changed. Neither, of course, is it any use to pretend that past events did not happen – it is exactly the tendency to repress painful experiences that leads to psychological dysfunction later in life. All the therapist or analyst can attempt to do is to expose the past, and allow it to be 'patterned' differently. In other words, brought out into the open, the adult mind is able to interpret that experience differently, and is therefore less influenced by the previous ways in which it has been interpreted, generally from the perspective of a young and vulnerable child.

Insight

As Heidegger and the Buddha pointed out, we live in three time zones: past, present and future. The past not only shapes what we are now, but is the source of the values and attitudes that will inform our choices for the future. But that process cannot be fixed and automatic, or therapy (to say nothing or ordinary discussion and persuasion) could never be effective. Clearly, what we see in therapy is the brain responding to, rather than initiating, the process of change. What does this say about eliminative materialism, or the general physicalist view of the mind?

Memory appears to work on a 'need to know' basis. We are not consciously aware of the whole of our past all the time; that would be to give our awareness an information overload. However, as we need to remember things – our name as we go to sign, where we have left the parked car, where we live, or where we had set out to go and the route by which to get there – so that information generally appears available to our conscious mind. An acting subject makes choices, behaves in predictable ways, and generally displays a particular identity, because of his or her memory. Predictability simply refers to the likelihood that a person will remember what has already happened and will act accordingly. The person who previously has disliked the taste of a certain food is likely to decline it when it is offered.

Returning to the consideration of therapy for a moment, all we need to see for our purposes here is that the way in which therapy works illustrates the function of memory as setting patterns of present interpretation. It is easiest to see this in the case of those who have been severely traumatized, and whose present life is hampered by those past events. But the process that is illustrated by therapy must surely apply to everyone – that our personal identity is shaped by the mapping and interpreting function (with past experiences giving us patterns for present interpretation), and the key to this is memory. We shall return to this 'mapping' function later, but first let us examine another common feature of our mental life – worrying.

Worrying

The ability to worry seems to be an interesting test of mind/body theories. The worrier is not concerned with actual situations, but with potential situations.

There is, or course, a logical cure for worrying: if something cannot be changed, then there seems to point in worrying about it, but if it can be changed, then there is still no point in worrying about it; one should simply set about changing it – a cure for anxiety put forward originally by the Stoics.

But that does not stop most people worrying. So what exactly is the worrier doing? Why can't he or she take the simple advice and recognize that worrying does not actually solve anything?

The worrier remembers past problems (or accounts of past problems given by others) and consequently anticipates similar problems in the future, turning the possibilities over and over in his or her mind. The worrier is said to be 'preoccupied', and the process of worrying can be quite exhausting. He or she might frown, or look distant, and it is clear that the source of that vagueness is not given by the present environment, or situation in which the person finds him or herself.

Now, a behaviourist might be tempted to identify worrying with the distant gaze, the knitted brow and the exhaustion and a compulsion to talk about what might happen. But if a behaviourist were right about mental actions being convenient names for material processes, then it would make no sense to say that someone was worried, but that he or she had completely disguised the fact. If observational data is all there is, there is no difference between 'looking worried' and 'being worried'. But we all know that it is possible to hide some of one's feelings and act calmly while living on the edge of panic – most actors about to go on stage could confirm that.

Worrying is also a problem for any epiphenomenal approach to mind. If mental states are simply a by-product of physical states, where does the worrying come from? It cannot be accounted for in terms of a response to present stimulus, since the cause of the worrying is imaginary – potential situations, rather than actual ones. Nor would it make sense to say that worrying is *produced* by exhaustion, a furrowed brow and so on.

But worrying does show the importance of the evolutionary function of mind. Thinking about how to deal with potentially difficult situations is, as we saw above (Chapter 3), a feature that gives members of a species a definite advantage, and therefore marks a direction for evolutionary advance. Worrying is an extreme version of the very technique that early man needed to develop in order to overcome problems – the ability to visualize potential situations and consider how to deal with them.

....

Insight

It seems clear to me that worrying is a feature of the whole person, not of the brain in isolation. Neurons can't 'worry'; they simply compute on the basis of stimulus, guided in this by having received similar stimulus in the past. And from a functionalist point of view, worrying is a pragmatist's nightmare – the *least* effective way of dealing with the problem in hand. Worrying is the inability to compute logically, and the inability to follow the course of action most advantageous in terms of natural selection. An automaton will always be more effective than a person who worries. If our minds are totally describable in terms of brain function, and that function has developed over millennia by natural selection, why have we developed the ability to worry?

....

Mapping our world

How do we develop our character? What makes us who we are? We have already looked at some of the factors involved – experience, memory, the situation into which we are 'thrown' at birth, our social networks, the values expressed by those around us that we either accept or reject. I want to suggest that there is an image that draws together the various strands of this process of becoming an individual and having an identity – *mapping*.

Most of what we do is automatic. We do not have to remember how to walk or eat; such skills operate through well-honed neural pathways. But we recognize people and our surroundings; we have a family life, or a career, or activities we enjoy. All these things are informed by memory, whether at a conscious or unconscious level. We experience who we are in relation to the personal world in which we live.

For each of us, our world is experienced as having values and meanings. People and places evoke memories, without which our nearest and dearest would be as strangers, we would have no idea where we lived or what we liked, or what we were able to do. We know that the brain is flexible and responds to particular experiences and use. We also know that it is the organ which enables memory to function. But how is this process of remembering and learning, which happens at a physical level in the brain, related to the way in which we develop as persons?

Consider this: you are a mental map, scaled 1:1 and superimposed over the world of your experience.

From the moment of birth, when as a baby you first cried out and sought a nipple or a bottle to meet your needs, your mind has been actively engaged in personalizing your world – this is where I find comfort, that is to be avoided, I know how to do this, I do not agree with that. Every moment of your waking life you are experiencing the world as shot through with meaning and significance; *you are experiencing a personal map*, overlaid onto the physical world of space and time.

Your map has been constructed and elaborated day by day through experience, and fixed by memory, both conscious and unconscious. Whatever you encounter, you experience 'as' and that 'as' is informed by memory. You carry out actions that are informed by previous practice – your neural pathways for them are well formed and facilitated by such practice.

Examples

When people gather – for a business meeting, perhaps, or a social event – each will come away from that occasion with a different interpretation of what has taken place. It will, for each of them, have a particular significance (or lack of it) in terms of their life, ambitions, likes, dislikes and so on. The objective fact of that meeting, which could be set out in great physical detail, would be the same for each of the participants. But because they are people and not impersonal monitoring devices, they will not experience it in the same way.

This obvious fact highlights the value of seeing each person in terms of their personal world map. Our society depends on the interlocking of many such maps. Falling in love may fuse parts of two maps, but for a good relationship the partners will need to keep other parts distinct. The act of domination is the attempt to destroy the victim's map, by appropriating all of his or her significance into their place in one's own.

What is it that gives you an identity? It is almost certainly some combination of the language you speak, the people you relate to, your views and dispositions, your personal history, your likes and dislikes, your habitual responses. None of these things are described *in terms of* brain function (even though we know that it is brain activity that makes it all possible); it is described in terms of *your world*. You are who you are because of the world within which you live, move and have your being.

It is a world that combines subjective and objective elements – space, time, matter and force, but also hopes, fears, places where you feel at home, people you love or fear. This is not the same as the world examined scientifically. That is a world where everything is seen as causally connected, located in space and time, having a particular mass and so on. Your brain is part of that world, but it is a category mistake to assume that 'you' operate exclusively on that level.

• •

Insight

The 'personal' world is formed by a process of experience that takes place *prior to* the split between objective and subjective. Once we ask whether such a world 'really' exists, and assume by that a world or space, time and causality, we have already started to eliminate the personal and the normative. They become 'subjective' and have nowhere in the world to exist. They may be in your mind, but they certainly do not exist in your brain. The idea that the self is an *object* is an illusion; but that does not mean that it is not *real*.

• •

In dreams, your map may become confused, typically mixing people and places from different periods of our life, until you wake and 'come to yourself' again. With amnesia, parts of the map become inaccessible to us; with dementia, parts may start to come apart. To a person suffering from such temporary or permanent degeneration we may say 'He's not himself or herself.' We are the map that we construct; it is what holds our life together.

Everything you do, even picking up and reading this book, is being related at every moment to the map of your life, its ideas checked against other things you may have read, or personal conclusions you have come to. Look around you and everything you see – whether familiar or strange – will be so in relation to your map. Nothing means anything to you until it is experienced 'as', until it is 'mapped'.

Insight

This is but the briefest sketch of my theory of personal mapping. It is set out in more detail in *Me* (Acumen Press, 2009).

To know someone, you need to see something of the personal 'map' that is their world. And if you doubt that, consider this: *If you want to know someone, which is more useful – a brain scan or a biography?*

Which brings us to the subject of our next chapter: knowledge of other minds.

10 THINGS TO KEEP IN MIND

1 The quest for identity is for something to give coherence to the process of change in life.

2 A collective entity can remain even if all its individual constituent parts change.

3 We are 'thrown' at birth into a particular set of circumstances that shape who we are.

4 Our identity may be established in terms of society and relationships.

5 We are shaped, consciously or unconsciously, by memory.

6 Memory tends to work on a 'need to know' basis.

7 Worrying is difficult to reconcile with a causally determined physicalist account of the self.

8 Our 'personalized' world is formed prior to the objective/subjective split.

9 From birth, you create a personal map to be superimposed 1:1 over your world.

10 Your personal identity is given in terms of the process of 'mapping' by which you engage with your world.

8

Knowledge of other minds

In this chapter you will:
- *consider whether you know anyone else*
- *doubt whether you know yourself*
- *wonder whether other people might be zombies.*

One of the most problematic implications of the dualist view of minds and bodies is that it leads to the strange conclusion that we cannot know minds other than our own. I *know* my own experiences and emotions immediately and directly, but (since the mind is not extended in time and space) all I can do is *infer* the minds of others. We tend to assume that we can know another person, because we can try to imagine what it must be to be that other person. But, in fact, all we have to go on is our experience of what they say or write; we cannot have direct access to their thoughts; we cannot engage with them directly at all. If the mind is separated off from the body, everything to do with knowing the minds of others becomes guesswork.

In terms of common experience, this is nonsense. We all understand what it means to know another person, or indeed to be misled about them, or to change our minds about them. This may be evidenced by what they say or do, but we are also convinced that we know 'them' as people.

All social interaction involves the interpretation of what others are thinking. Why is he doing that? What is she looking for? And that becomes more precise when language and writing are involved. We hear or read what others think – and often have to interpret in order to see what they mean, or use our imaginations to see tease out unspoken implications. We know that other people have minds, not simply by analogy with our experience of our own minds, but because we share in a common experience. I would not have my thoughts or language were it not for other people.

That being the case, we have to assume that there is something wrong with any dualistic theory that puts the knowledge of other people into question. But it equally challenges a simplistic reduction of the mind to the activity of neurons, since we do not require the presence of an fMRI scanner at every social event – communication is between minds, not between brains, even if the latter are making the former possible. So, however detailed and precise my knowledge about the neural activity of the person I am encountering, it is never going to be *the same as* that other person's *experience*. To return to the familiar image: you cannot discover the purpose of a journey by examining the workings of a motorcar engine.

In this way the problem of how we know other minds becomes a good way of sorting out what we mean by mind and how it relates to the physical body.

The structuralist approach

Early psychologists – for example Wilhelm Wundt (1932–20) in Germany and Edward Titchener (1967–1927), who helped to establish experimental psychology in the United States – hoped to understand the structure of the mind, and to explain it in physical terms. They were generally opposed to the Cartesian dualism that made the mind inaccessible to physical investigation, and wanted to show that thinking was essentially a physical process.

These psychologists assumed that the process of thinking was based on images, and that images came from simple sensations. Hence, if the process of thought could be analysed into the very simplest of sensations, its structure could be revealed. But how were these sensations to be known? Clearly, the only way was for people to describe what they experienced, breaking down that experience into its component parts.

The process of doing this was laborious. The people giving their descriptions could not simply say that they saw, for example a red flower. Rather, they had to break down exactly the quality of colour, shape, smell, touch and so on that added up to the overall experience of the flower. The assumption was made that the mind simply put all these simple sensations together in order to construct the concept 'red flower'.

But there was a huge problem with this whole approach. It depended upon the skill of the person being interviewed in being able to analyse experience accurately. What was more, there seemed to be way of checking the accuracy of their accounts. What if they were mistaken? What if they were lying? What (as often happened) if two people gave different analyses of identical stimuli?

In the end, these 'structuralists', as they became known, listed 44,000 elementary sensations, but their whole task failed because there was no way of knowing if any of them was in fact correct. The psychologists were totally dependent upon what the subjects said to them. They had no other way of knowing if the person had actually had a particular sensation. Introspection was their only method of working, because only the person actually having that sensation could possibly know and describe it. Nobody else was in a position to challenge that because nobody else could know what was going on in that person's mind.

It was against that background that the behaviourists (e.g. Pavlov, Watson and Skinner) presented stimulus and response as the basis of their work. Responses could be observed and measured in a way that allowed psychology to follow the norms of the physical sciences. They were no longer dependent upon unconfirmable reports from an experiencing subject, since their subjects now exhibited patterns of behaviour that could be measured.

Hence, behaviourism thought that it had got round the problem of knowledge of other minds by saying, in effect, that there should be no reference to 'internal' states of mind at all. Psychology was concerned only with the prediction of observable behaviour – of how people and animals learned and responded to things. Whatever 'thought' might have taken place between stimulus and response was irrelevant. What counted was what could be observed. For them, consciousness either did not exist, or – if it did – it was an epiphenomenon (see Chapter 2), produced by brain activity.

Hence, the problem of the knowledge of other minds (or rather, the impossibility of observing the workings of another mind) shaped much of the early development of psychology as a science.

....

Insight

Science depends upon evidence, and if there is no way of gaining independently checkable and objective evidence about the workings of the mind, then there can be no science of mind. That was the fundamental problem facing the structuralist and behaviourist approaches to psychology.

....

Other people's brains

Everyone agrees that, when mental activity is going on, there is also physical activity also going on in that person's brain. To describe someone as 'brain dead' indicates that there is absolutely no brain function (which could be measured, since it involves electrical activity) and therefore that there is no chance of a return to consciousness.

We saw earlier that a materialist/physicalist viewpoint is one that identifies mental operations with brain activity. But this viewpoint does not solve a fundamental problem, the classical account of which is known as 'Leibniz's gap' (see Chapter 2).

In section 17 of his short work *Monadology*, Leibniz considers the problem of how one might examine the process of perception. He argues that perception cannot be described in terms of a mechanism. Even if one could construct a mechanism that could think and feel, on examining that mechanism it would be like – in his analogy – entering a mill. One would see only pieces of mechanism that push against one another – but one would not be able to see the thought or sensation itself.

....

Insight

In other words, there is always going to be a gap between the concepts we use in describing physical mechanisms and those we use to describe thought and sensation, and that gap is going to remain, even if we achieve a perfect neuroscience.

....

Thus, even if we were convinced that thought was identical to brain activity, the language used to describe that activity would not be the same as that which describes thought. Language about mental activity cannot be reduced to that about brain function, even if it is shown that the brain function is the sole and sufficient condition for a mental operation taking place.

This has immediate implications for the considerations of both brains and artificially constructed brains in the form of computers. Even if we have a computer which appears to 'think' the thoughts are not the same as the operations of that computer. There will always be a gap between saying that this is what the computer is doing, and saying what (or if) the computer is thinking. Hence, unless you are an eliminative materialist (see Chapter 4) and believe that they are one and the same thing, *even a full and detailed knowledge of neurobiology would not allow you to know what it is like to experience the workings of another mind.* Science thus enables us to examine other people's brains and even to intervene, surgically or pharmacologically, in the activity of those brains, but it cannot show what it is like to be those people.

Ways of knowing

Taking a dualistic view of minds and bodies, it is impossible to have direct knowledge of another mind. You can get to know a person well, understanding his or her words, actions, writings and body language, but you cannot get direct access to his or her mind. If, following Descartes, minds are unextended, knowledge of other minds cannot come through sense experience, but must be inferred by analogy with one's own experience of being a conscious human being.

Of course, if you turn from dualism and follow the views of Gilbert Ryle, there is no problem. There is no 'ghost in the machine': what we mean by 'mind' is the intelligent and communicative abilities of that other person. It is a description of what they do and say. If I know his or her actions, words and so on, then I know his or her mind; the two things are one and the same.

But self-knowledge is always going to be a problem for those who follow Ryle's view. If mental phenomena are simply covert ways of describing physical actions or dispositions to act, then my knowledge of myself is not qualitatively different from my knowledge of others. I notice that I have smiled, and therefore come to the conclusion that it is appropriate to call myself 'happy'. I find myself jumping up and down and holding my leg, and I assume that I have suffered 'pain'.

This, of course, is nonsense. Those physical actions are made in response to a subjective experience. Where other people are concerned, because I cannot have direct access to their subjective experiences, I have to infer them from the resulting actions, gestures words and so on. In my own case, however, the subjective experience is not inferred from anything, it is experienced directly.

To justify saying that someone else is happy, one needs empirical evidence – of smiling, or saying that he or she is happy, of skipping down the road or whatever. That evidence, by analogy with one's own experience, gives one reasonable grounds for saying that the other person is 'happy'.

Insight

Notice that we are dealing here with evidence and the grounds for the ascription of mental predicates. We should always take care to distinguish *what* we know from *how* we know it. We may know the feelings of another person by observing their behaviour, but that does not imply that their feelings are *identical* to their behaviour. Observation is a way of knowing, not the content of what is known.

But, clearly, language is shared, and a word needs to have the same meaning when applied to others as well as to oneself. This led P.F. Strawson (particularly in an article entitled 'Persons' in 1958) to argue that the concept of a person or individual is a *primitive* one. If the same thing can be predicated of others on the basis of observable evidence, and of myself on the basis of subjective experience, then there must be a sense of the person that is deeper than the conventional subject/object distinction. In other words, the idea of person includes *both* the physical *and* the non-physical. Once the idea of person is placed centrally in this debate, then the use of language both for myself and others makes more sense – its ascription can use different criteria, but its meaning remains constant. (This type of argument in favour of a primitive notion of 'person' had also been put forward by A.J. Ayer in *The Concept of a Person*, 1955.)

Predicates that imply a person 'is happy', for example, go beyond those that simply give a physical description (e.g. 'is thin'), in that they presuppose that the object to which we ascribe them has states of consciousness.

In other words, although the ways of knowing are very different, we have a primitive sense of a person, which justifies the ascription of personal predicates both to ourselves and to others. I know when I am in pain, and I see when someone else is in pain – and the reasons for knowing it are very different in the two cases – but, if we hold that the idea of 'person' is primitive, then we may assume that to say that you are in pain and that I am in pain refer to the same experience.

Insight

That may seem obvious now, but at a time when justification for ascribing predicates (and the dominance of linguistic philosophy in general) was paramount, it broke the impasse of having very different criteria for ascribing the same predicates to oneself and to others.

There are other possible ways to know another mind. One of these it *telepathy*, and the detailed arguments about whether or not it is possible are beyond the scope of this book. It may be that there is some direct but unconscious way of ascertaining what another person is thinking. Certainly, there is evidence that some people, particularly close relatives, claim such knowledge, and such evidence needs to be assessed on exactly the same terms as any other scientific hypothesis. Or it may be that what passes for telepathy is in fact a form of fast and unconscious intuition from the conscious or unconscious visual clues that the other person gives to the content of his or her mind.

More obvious than intuition is the fact that, in the ordinary run of things, we generally know other people through *language*. We know what they are thinking, and indeed that they are capable of thought, because they tell us. Sometimes we have a problem, in that the person we want to get to know cannot speak our language. We may have to make do with sign language. Similarly with higher forms of animal life – a dog may know a few words and may respond, by wagging its tail, or skulking away sheepishly, according to whether it identifies our words as of praise or blame.

But how can we tell whether another person has a process of thinking that is like our own? I have a string of words going through my head. Do others have the same? Generally speaking, except for moments when we just sit and stare, we have words and concepts, running in our minds. What would it be like to have a mind but no language? Could we think without language of some sort?

If language is the necessary medium through which the process of reflective consciousness takes place, other questions are raised:

▶ Which comes first, the rational mind or language?
▶ In other words, do we grow mentally through using language and communication, or do we evolve intelligent consciousness and only then put it to good use in communication and language?

It is clear that the development of mind has gone hand in hand with the increase in brain volume. But which has produced which? Is mental development something that takes place *between* people rather than simply in their heads? If so, the phenomenon of the evolutionary increase in brain capacity is simply the result of an increase in the population of those who have an advantage in the breeding and survival stakes through the use of greater brainpower and therefore more effective communication.

Insight

Another way of putting this would be to say that we do not communicate better because we have a larger brain, but that we develop a larger brain because we need to communicate better.

If language and communication – with all the social advantages that have come with them – are the key to the increase in mental capacity, then the computer model of mind is rather lacking. There is no point in building bigger and bigger computers in the hope that eventually the processors will rival the human brain, and then suddenly expect it to be brilliant. Clearly, the process of developing brilliance requires shared communication. To be cut off from the world of thought and language is to be stunted. Hence the 'mental' world need not be located between the ears. True, that is the locus of each individual's experienced share of the mental world, but the mental activity itself is far from physically located. The individual thinking alone may be private now, but the activity of thinking is not separable from the rest of the world – for all the concepts being used in those private thoughts have been acquired socially; that is the nature of language.

Since the experience of consciousness includes much of the 'inner dialogue' of thought, as well as those moments when we are actually speaking or writing, it is clear that our most private thoughts are borrowed from the public domain. Society and language provide our principle way of knowing, or certainly of sharing our knowledge.

Zombies

What would happen if you could use a machine to duplicate every cell in your body, and in effect create what appeared to be another person physically identical to yourself, with all the usual functions of movement and so on, but with no conscious experience? Such a being is referred to in philosophical discussions as a zombie. Now the key question is this: *How can you tell the difference between a zombie and a normal human being?* In other words, how – once you have given a full physical description (which would be identical for you and you zombie) – do you start to describe the *person*?

Of course, if zombies are literally possible, then the case for dualism is complete – for one could show exactly what it is like to have all the physical attributes but without a mind. But, surely, even if it is possible simply to *imagine* what a zombie would be like (and, surely, everyone can do that), then it implies that we actually understand people in dualist terms.

Mindless!

We all have a notion of what a mindless dummy would be like, and if we are cruel enough to refer to a work colleague in this way, we know what sort of characteristics (or lack of them) has led us to make the comment! So, whether or not we agree with the philosophical arguments in favour of dualism, for practical purposes we do know how to assess mental qualities (or lack of them) on the basis of observation of bodies and the words issuing from them.

Of course, the kind of dualism that the dummy illustrates could well be a dualism of properties, rather than of essences. The mindless dummy behind that desk has a complete set of physical properties and a total absence of mental ones.

Now there is a clear distinction between thinking that it should be possible for something to exist and knowing that it exists. I may have an idea of a zombie – for all the reasons given above – but that does not mean that a zombie actually exists. So how can I tell if the apparently human object in front of me is a person or a zombie?

A zombie, in the philosophical sense, is physically identical to a normal human being. Thus every conceivable test that could be put to the zombie would be returned as if done by a normal human. But what the zombie does not have, apparently, is the inner experience of a mind – *but that is unobservable anyway*.

The argument that, because we can conceive of a zombie existing, we must accept some form of dualism, actually amounts to this:

▶ You can experience your own mind.
▶ You cannot experience someone else's mind.
▶ Someone else's mind is only known in so far as it is mediated by language or action.
▶ Such mediation is equally open to zombies, if the zombie is programmed accordingly.
▶ Therefore it is no more possible to prove that this thing in front of you is a zombie that to prove that it is an intelligent human being.

The zombie argument is a thought experiment, showing how very different our ideas of mind and matter are. But that is all it amounts to. In the real world, we could never know if zombies exist, for (other than in our imagination) we have no independent knowledge of other minds.

Insight

By the same token, we cannot know *what it is like* to be an animal; it is possible to see animals as automata, in effect as zombies, and that is what some people claim. However, if it is logically impossible, on the evidence of the senses, to tell a well-programmed zombie from a conscious human being, it must be equally impossible to tell whether an animal has conscious experience or not. And if our general assumption is that other living human beings do have consciousness, it is equally valid to assume that animals do, too.

Let us return for a moment to our consideration of artificial intelligence (see Chapter 3). In the end, artificial intelligence makes what is, in effect, a rather banal contribution to issues of the nature of self and consciousness. Namely that, given the ability to make a computer with the same capacity as the human brain, and given input sensors and output devices equal to those of human senses and bodily functions, then that computer (embodied in a robot, in order to receive and respond to stimuli) would be indistinguishable from a human person.

But what has been achieved by this? A zombie. To claim that it might be possible to produce an exact replica of a human being, and then say that such a replica would be indistinguishable from the original, is to make a hypothetical claim that, in effect, can yield nothing by way of information about the self other than what can be gained by observing ordinary human beings.

It would be necessary, of course, to give the replica a history, complete with memories. It would also take as long to produce it as it is to grow a human being, so that the replica can gradually learn and experience every stage of life.

In other words – if one could make a human being, exactly as human beings are made, then the result would be indistinguishable from human beings. But of course! And the problem of whether such a replica was actually a person, or had consciousness like any ordinary human person, would be no different from our present questions about the knowledge of other minds. The only difference would be that we might assume that we had solved the problem, because we assume that, if we have a perfect analysis and reconstruction of something, we must therefore have *understood* it. That is simply not the case; analysis does not reveal the complexity of organisms, only the various operations of the parts of which they are composed.

Insight

It seems to be that the issue of whether it might be possible to understand human identity and mind by a process of constructing a replica human being, with all the background that would be required, comes down to this: 'If we were able to construct a world exactly like this one, then it would be exactly like this one.' Which, as a contribution to the understanding of mind, is trivial.

Are we alone?

Clearly, if the only mind we can know directly is our own, then we may doubt that any other mind exists, since all we can experience of others is what our senses detect in terms of their bodies, gestures, words and actions. We cannot touch other minds directly and may therefore doubt their existence. Such a lonely view is termed *solipsism*, and this is the fate of those who think of the mind as an unknowable 'ghost' – the caricature of Descartes that Ryle presented.

But what does this really mean? I cannot know exactly what it is like to be that other person as I cannot have that person's experiences, but to suggest that implies that I cannot know another mind is to limit the mind to the most obvious of dualist caricatures – the private, unknowable world between the other person's ears.

We may look another person in the eyes and sense we are looking into their deepest thoughts, probing for signs of sincerity or duplicity. But what is actually there, behind those eyes? Nothing but the soft grey matter of the brain. And all the possible scientific equipment available will do no more than show in what parts of that grey matter energy is being used.

At one level, therefore, the solipsist argument seems to have force. The world I experience is not the same as my experiencing of it; and if someone else examined me at this moment, they would not be able to 'see' what I am experiencing, only the physical organs that enable me to do so. Therefore, although solipsism seems quite unacceptable, the argument in favour of it is quite straightforward and logical. Happiness is not the same thing as smiling; I assume that others are happy, but I may be fooled. Any actor could present to me a completely bogus set of mental characteristics.

Insight

Shakespeare saw all the world as a stage. True, I may stand upon it and play the various parts I am given, and others do the same. The tragedy is that, if solipsism is true, we only ever know the parts others play, never our fellow actors. The play continues, but all the others could be puppets for all I know, and I a puppet as they observe me. And if, frustrated by this, I step out of role and make a personal appeal to them, they will assume that I have merely adopted yet another role.

Hence there is no way that I can know another mind for certain. I merely look out at the world of my experience and, by analogy, assume that other bodies represent persons with minds. But that fate only highlights the falseness of the quest to locate the self in some invisible, private world within the skull.

I know that I am a person and that I have a mind, the problem is how I might convince someone else of that fact. They hear my words, see my actions, with MRI they can even see the workings of my brain. But how can I explain to them that all this is me?

Knowing me

It is a feature of dualism that one has immediate and certain knowledge of one's own mind, but not of other people's. This is the 'privileged access' view that was attacked by Gilbert Ryle. However, just because – following Descartes – I am aware of myself as a thinking being and cannot be persuaded that I do not exist while I am aware of my own thoughts, it does not follow that I can *define* myself simply in those terms. I may be forced to acknowledge that I am a thinking being, but I sense that I am a lot more besides.

Not all philosophers were as certain about themselves as Descartes. Both Hume and Kant, when they tried to interrogate their own minds, found only a procession of particular thoughts and experiences. The self generally remained *elusive*. In other words, it is clear that parts of me may be amputated without altering my sense of identity; I can speak of 'my hand' or 'my foot'. But I can also speak of 'my body' and 'my mind' with the implication that neither physical nor mental aspects of myself can be *all* that I am.

This should not be surprising. Just as Nagel challenged us to think about what it might be like to be a bat, and showed that a description was not the same as 'what it was like to be', so it is obvious that the various bits and pieces of myself are part of a description (they *objectify* parts of me – looking at them, as it were, from the outside), and therefore cannot show 'what it is like to be me'.

However, even if other people cannot know what I am thinking, that does not necessarily imply that the content of my thoughts is exclusively my own. We may have privileged access to the way we are thinking about and valuing the phenomena that we are experiencing, but that does not mean that our experiences are unique. Indeed, if we start to describe them, we do so using language that is shared. Even the way we describe something to ourselves, in our inner dialogue, we use concepts that have been learned from other people. Without shared language, our head is silent.

Therefore, when people speak of 'privileged access' we need to remember that there is a difference between the fact that we alone can get *access* to what we are thinking, and the *content* of that thinking; the former is known only through introspection, but the latter is produced socially and only makes sense in a shared environment.

Are you in my world?

One thing is abundantly clear at this stage in the argument: any attempt to give an objective description of the self as 'I' is going to end in frustration. Whenever we try to describe ourselves, the 'I' vanishes from that description. As we saw above, I can speak of 'my mind', 'my emotions' as well as 'my body'. There is always an 'I' of 'what it is like to be me' that is over and above whatever is being described. *I stand back from whatever is in my world, even if I acknowledge it as 'mine'.*

But if other people cannot directly experience the 'I' that is more than my body, with its words and its actions, then neither can they be part of the world that I experience. I cannot know them directly. In other words, the self – whether that's yourself or myself – is not 'in' the world as a separate, identifiable entity. This is a claim made by Ludwig Wittgenstein. In his famous work *Tractatus Logico-Philosophicus* he examines the meaning of statements in terms of the way they correspond to entities in the physical world, and argued that:

> **'The philosophical I is not the man, not the human body or the human soul of which psychology treats, but the metaphysical subject, the limit – not part of the world.'**
>
> *Tractatus* 5.641

For Wittgenstein, 'The World is all that is the case' – in other words, our language pictures the external world, so that the limits of our language are also the limits of our world. But the thought that we are not part of the world has its positive side, since it implies that death is not part of my world; *we never actually experience our own death*. At death, we simply cease to experience; we cannot get 'outside' the situation and look back in and see ourselves dead.

However much we might want to, the plain fact is that we cannot get outside the world and look back in! Our language refers to this world that we experience here and now. So, if the subject self is not part of the world, we cannot speak or even think about it directly:

> **'What we cannot think, that we cannot think: we cannot therefore say what we cannot think.'**
>
> *Tractatus* 5.61

Tractatus is a notoriously difficult book, because its strings of short, numbered aphorisms require a great deal of unpacking to yield their full meaning. What we can say, however, is that Wittgenstein has probed the limits of what can be said meaningfully. The world is coextensive with what we can think, know and say. We cannot set its limits, because we cannot get outside it to observe those limits. We do know, however, that in a real sense 'we' are not part of our world – the philosophical 'self' is the *limit* of the world.

Some philosophers (e.g. Paul Churchland) argue that we do not actually come to know other minds by means of analogy, nor as the result of some deductive conclusion from experience, but simply because the assumption that there are other minds, similar to our own, is a *reasonable explanatory hypothesis*. In other words, if you assume it to be the case, then it makes it reasonably straightforward to predict the behaviour of other people. If you do not assume that there are other minds, then you have to go through some fairly complicated sorts of reasoning in order to determine how you should treat people who are known to the senses, but whose minds remain unknown to you.

So, to the question 'Are you in my world?' the most sensible answer is that – although I cannot experience what it is like to be you – the most straightforward assumption to make is that you exist and express yourself though language and action, just as I do. You cannot be defined as any one thing in the world of my experience. You are not exclusively identified with nerve endings, or neurons, or the ever-changing physical body that I identify as yours.

Your 'self' will never be found in the world that is examinable by science – the physical, material world. However much I seek to know you, your experiencing self will always elude my grasp. Your brain can be in my world; I can watch an MRI scan and see it working away, but that is not the same as seeing you. On the other hand, if I assume – as a working hypothesis – that you are a living, sensing, experiencing subject self, then I can test out that hypothesis by speaking to you! And, once there is a conversation going, my hypothesis is confirmed and we can get to know one another.

10 THINGS TO KEEP IN MIND

1 The structuralists tried to understand the mind by listing all the elements that go to make up experience.

2 Behaviourism avoided the problem of other minds by denying internal states.

3 Leibniz acknowledged that no mechanism could explain perception.

4 We have 'privileged access' to the content of our own minds.

5 A zombie is physically identical to a human being but without an experiencing self.

6 Solipsism is the view that we cannot know other minds.

7 The self is elusive, known by thought but not defined as thought.

8 Wittgenstein saw the self as the limit of the world.

9 We cannot objectively define what it is like to be us.

10 The existence of other minds, although not provable, is a reasonable hypothesis.

9

....

Free will and ethics

In this chapter you will:
- *consider whether your every action is determined by physical causes*
- *examine how actions relate to beliefs*
- *explore the ethical implications of theories of mind.*

If my mind is no more than a by-product of processes going on in my brain, or if the eliminative materialist or behaviourist understanding of the mind is correct, then whatever I do is determined by the same process of cause and effect that operates throughout the physical universe. But does that square with my own experience? And do I see others as totally conditioned by their physical circumstances, or as free agents? And if none of us has the freedom to choose what we do, can we be held morally responsible?

The issue of free will is a key one in the philosophy of mind, touching on issues concerned with science, religion and ethics. To a large measure, my understanding of freedom and morality will colour my understanding of the nature of the self.

Freedom and physical causality

I decide to do something, and then do it. That is a most obvious feature of sentient life; our thoughts lead to actions. But how it that possible?

This question was posed in May 1643 by Princess Elizabeth of Bohemia, writing to her illustrious tutor, Descartes, asking him to explain how it could be that the mind, being only a thinking substance, could affect any movement in the body, since the latter is the result the thing moved being pushed, and that requires contact and extension – neither of which apply to the mind as Descartes had described it. The royal student had put her finger on the weak point of Descartes' theory.

The problem is that, in any scientific analysis of physical nature, the chain of causality spreads outwards and backwards from any physical event; everything arises in dependence upon other things, and there appear to be no 'gaps' in the chain of causation into which the 'mental' input can be inserted. The physical world seems to be seamless and to give a complete explanation of action, without the need for minds at all.

One thing that needs to be appreciated here is how very limited Descartes' concept of physical causation was. We should not assume that Descartes had what was to become the later Newtonian view of science. Far from it. His mechanics depended upon contact. Thus 'A' could only influence 'B' if there could be shown to be some direct physical contact between them. Newtonian physics, by contract, accepted the idea of forces, namely the influence of bodies upon one another through fields of force, acting at a distance. Hence, in looking at issues of freedom, and thus of the mechanisms by which mental activity can influence physical activity, we should not be concerned to find a replacement for the pineal gland – even Newtonian physics went beyond that. Does Newtonian physics leave open the possibility that the mind may also be a non-material cause of movement? After all, you can't 'observe' gravity.

Gravity

Gravity does not 'exist' in the sense of being an object among other objects. Gravity is simply the way of describing a force that acts between bodies, itself the product of the size and proximity of those bodies. Therefore, there wouldn't be gravity holding me down, if it were not for the fact that I am a small physical body standing on a much larger physical body, namely the planet. But the 'gravity', which describes that downward force, is not a 'third' material thing over above the planet and my physical body.

Thinking of mental causation as an invisible force, like gravity, may at least get rid of the cruder images of causal chains without gaps. But, of course, it does not address the key problem, which is that gravity is still a physically measurable force, while the subject self – from the dualist perspective – does not appear in any measurable way within the physical world. We should also note that Newton claimed (disputable, but we need not go into that) not to frame hypotheses as to the cause of what he observed, but only deduce physical laws from his observations. We can observe and measure human behaviour – just as the behaviourists did – but do we then go on to frame the hypothesis of a subject self causing that behaviour?

However, as science has developed it is generally accepted that there are only four basic forces, the strong and weak nuclear, the electromagnetic and gravity, and that one or more of these forces must cause all physical movement. Hence the idea of 'vital spirits' or the like has generally been rejected, along with the idea that a special force 'emerges' from specific, complex arrangements of matter in the brain and nervous systems of sentient beings.

Which brings us back to Descartes' problem – that we still have to find some way in which mental activity can lead to physical activity. A very clear definition (and one which relates closely to his overall thesis about the failure of Descartes' dualism) comes from Gilbert Ryle in *The Concept of Mind*:

> **'The problem of the Freedom of the Will was the problem how to reconcile the hypothesis that minds are to be described in terms drawn from the categories of mechanics with the knowledge that higher-grade human conduct is not of a piece with the behaviour of machines.'**

In other words, what Ryle (and others) have pointed out is that human activity becomes problematic if we use the analogy of the machine to try to understand human activity, and therefore try to find some way of getting an *additional causal factor* into the mechanistic chain, a factor which will allow people a measure of freedom in what they do.

The main thing to avoid in this discussion is the temptation to see the body as a mechanistic chain that needs to have just *one more* causal factor within it, for that would send us off on the quest for a modern version of Descartes' pineal gland.

The other thing to observe is that the mind *influences but does not determine* physical action. I may, for example, choose to fly, or to jump 30 feet into the air – but choosing to do so is as far as I am able to get with either aspiration. There are always going to be physical constraints. Whatever is done is in line with the normal actions of physical bodies. The effect of the mind is to select between the almost infinite number of *possible* physical actions that can take place.

Thus, I choose which word to utter. My tongue is equally physically capable of articulating 'Yes' or 'No'. In terms of physical causation, there is nothing to choose between them. With hindsight – and the benefit of total knowledge of all the physical, neural, linguistic and social factors involved – we can show that either 'Yes' or 'No' was inevitable. But in anticipation, perhaps involving worrying and the desperate weighing of imagined results, we experience the freedom to choose between them.

Told you so!

Even if the tongue is capable of either reply, and the scientific understanding of the action permits either word, there is still a sense in which my reply may be determined. That is, someone who knows me well, having observed my replies to questions on many other occasions, may be able to predict accurately whether I will reply 'Yes' or 'No'. In other words, we may be psychologically or sociologically determined.

But we have already seen that the sense of personal identity and individual character is built up through the accumulation of experience and the patterns of understanding and evaluation that come from them. Such patterning and evaluation are integral to the way we experience the world. The question is: *Are those patterns of*

*understanding etched into our neural pathways, such that they
cannot but influence future experience?* If so, one might be able to
make a case for neural determinism, where each experience reshapes
neural networks and therefore reshapes the way future experience is
received and responded to.

Modern science does not have a predetermined concept of what
counts as our 'body'. Rather, 'body' is whatever is discovered to be
physically the case. The scientist does not draw a line and suggest
that everything beyond it must have some occult cause, to be found
in a quasi-mechanical but non-extended mental realm. Rather,
whatever phenomenon is observed becomes a valid object of study.
Just because a set of physical actions – e.g. language, accompanied
by gestures of movements – is explicable only in terms of the overall
life of a complex being that displays features of consciousness and
volition, does not make it occult. Any explanation may require new
concepts or a new approach, but such 'mental' actions should be, in
principle, explicable.

How them might any such explanation square with the experience of
freedom?

UNCERTAINTY AND MICROTUBES – DEAD END OR WAY OUT?

Just as Cartesian mechanics gave way to Newtonian physics, that has
given way to relativity and quantum mechanics, and it is therefore
tempting (but probably, in the long run, unproductive) to look to the
new physics for some way out of the freedom/determinism problem.

Quantum theory shows that, at the subatomic level, there is
fundamental uncertainty; everything remains in a wave form, with
its precise location indeterminate, until observed. Once observed, the
wave collapses into some definite state or other. Thus you have an
element of freedom and randomness, in place of the older Newtonian
physics of fixed physical laws. Is it possible that consciousness resides
is some such level within the brain, below the level of neurons?

It has been observed that all living cells have protein structures made
up of microtubes, and that these may be related to what we know

as consciousness. The fact that, like subatomic particles, they may be indeterminate until accessed, led Roger Penrose to suggest that human freedom might be explained in terms of such microtubes. If so, freedom creeps in at the bottom run of the physical ladder. But that hardly does justice to the experience of freedom operating at the level of the whole complex entity.

It is also true that even strictly deductive systems, like mathematics, cannot ever prove all their basic assumptions. There comes a point at which the explanation of fundamental principles remains incomplete, complete proof is impossible – this was put forward by Kurt Gödel, and is generally referred to as 'Gödel's theorem'.

Insight

Since quantum mechanics has shown fundamental indeterminism, and shattered the certainties of the older Newtonian physics, and since Gödel has shown that not even mathematics can sort out its own foundations completely, it is tempting to see both areas as opening the way for a kind of indeterminacy that will allow mental activity to have an impact on the physical world.

In practice, however, this is not very helpful. The quantum theorist Erwin Schrödinger (famous for his 'Schrödinger's Cat' thought experiment) pointed out that quantum indeterminacy operates only at the subatomic level. At the level of human beings, the quantum approach is simply not appropriate.

Just because mathematics is not totally self-justifying, or subatomic particles predictable, that does not stop 2 + 2 = 4 from remaining true, or challenge the speed of acceleration of a ball rolling down a slope. Thus we may indeed find that there is quantum indeterminacy in microtubes, but that is not necessarily relevant at the level of individual mental activity and its resulting physical action.

In modern debate, the issue of how the mind can initiate bodily action can be used to support a materialist or physicalist viewpoint. If physical effects need to have physical causes, and if we accept the obvious fact that mental states can being about physical changes, then those mental states *must themselves be physical.*

So does this give us a way out of the problem? We are concerned with the way in which human beings interact with their environment, and the fact that they experience free will in doing so. Both they and their environment may be described physically – but just as physical indeterminism operates at the subatomic level, but not at the level of whole human beings, so we are most unlikely to find that the experience of freedom can profitably be linked with the unpredictability of microtubes.

Just as Descartes conveniently chose as his explanation (the pineal gland) something that, at the time, was remarkably inaccessible to examination, but well located, so microtubes, or any other theory that might emerge in terms of the level of physical reality below that of our individual neurons, are conveniently inaccessible and therefore manage to push the problem further away from us – as something that we might be able to understand one day. My guess, however, is that when it comes to an explanation for the experience of human freedom, such a quest is likely to be more of a dead end than a way out.

FREEDOM AS AN ILLUSION

Spinoza took the view that everything in the world was totally determined by physical causes (see Chapter 2), and that there was therefore no scope for human freedom. And this, of course, has been the approach of materialists and behaviourists, who have also tried to fit the idea of mind into a closed system of physical cause and effect, or to identify the mind exclusively with neural activity.

But if this is the case, why is it that we have the illusion of freedom? How can I so easily be fooled into thinking that I have choice, or that I make a difference as I type these words into my computer? Why do I sense that I am responsible for what I do?

Spinoza's answer is that we simply do not understand all the complex sets of causes that determine what happens. Now this is clear enough. We know some causes and physical limitations. If I sense that I am launching myself from a window and gently floating on the wind, I know that I am dreaming, for unaided flight is a physical impossibility for human beings. But I have to accept that I do not know *all* the possible influences upon my actions. Thus, for example, my therapist would be quick to point out causes of my actions of which I was quite unaware. Many influences from my past, long forgotten, may shape my present action.

The approach taken by Spinoza is therefore reasonable as far as it goes. If I knew absolutely everything there is to know, then I would know that there are very good reasons for every apparently 'free' decision I make. The fact that I can be indecisive, or that I think I am making a completely free choice, simply reflects my ignorance.

THE EXPERIENCE OF FREEDOM

Kant distinguished between things as we experience them (*phenomena*) and things as they are in themselves (*noumena*). When I examine anything in the world, I do so in terms of categories of thought, including space, time and causality. Every object is determined by these categories, because that is the way our minds deal with objects. So we cannot see objects (including observed human objects) as free agents because our minds automatically impose causality on our interpretation of their action.

Using that same distinction, I can *experience* my own freedom. I do so, not as an 'object' of someone else's experience, but as a 'noumenal' subject. If I tried to look at myself as an object, as I might do if being asked to explain the course of my career for example, then I would try to explain the influences upon me. If radically honest, I would present myself as an object. But that would not be the way I had actually lived my life; each choice along the way would have expressed my own experience of freedom.

Kant argued that we are, *at one and the same time*, phenomenally conditioned and noumenally free.

ACTIONS, INTENTIONS AND BELIEFS

We do what we do because of our beliefs. If I am thirsty and believe that there is a beer in the fridge, I will go over and open the fridge door. The belief (about the beer) leads to the action – in other words there is a 'predictive strategy' based on that belief. The belief is real enough, and can presumably be identified with a certain pattern of brain behaviour, but it is only known because of the *intentional* nature of conscious behaviour. (For intentionality, see also Chapter 5.)

But the implication of an intentionalist stance is that mind plays an *instrumental* role in human life. It is there for a purpose, and that purpose is not simply the passive one of receiving and understanding information conveyed by the senses. It enables us to interpret, understand and engage with the world around us. It enables us to translate beliefs into intentions and intentions into actions. The eye, optic nerve and neural areas processing sight are not an end in themselves, neither are they simply the way we receive information; they are the means by which we look and find our way around. Here is Friedrich Nietzsche on the mind:

> **'What the sense feels, what the spirit perceives, is never an end in itself. But sense and spirit would like to persuade you that they are the end of all things: they are as vain as that.'**

> **'Sense and spirit are instruments and toys: behind them still lies the Self [my emphasis]. The Self seeks with the eyes of the senses; it listens too with the ears of the spirit.'**

> *Thus Spoke Zarathustra*

Thus, for Nietzsche, the Self is not the same thing as consciousness. Feelings and thoughts are the vehicles for getting things done, not ends in themselves. The Self is that which acts and has goals, which seeks to develop itself and move forward. This is what it means to be a conscious, living being. In the case of humankind, of course, the self can call upon a rich array of mental and emotional tools with which to express itself and forward its aims in life.

I sense that, if Nietzsche were asked if we were free to act (following some discussion of the problem of freedom and determinism), he would probably say that action is determined by the Self, with both body and mind as the necessary instruments for doing so. Is freedom possible then? Only for those who have the courage of their convictions!

If the brain and nervous system is examined as a machine – albeit the most complex machine possible – then it cannot be normative. Values and meanings do not exist at the level of electrochemical exchanges. This is absolutely crucial if we are to prevent the madness of trying to reduce the significance of human action to the level of brain activity, and nowhere is this seen more clearly than in the area of ethics.

Ethics and the brain

Are we morally responsible? If freedom is an illusion and everything is physically determined, then we have no choice about what we do. In that case, it makes little sense to say that actions are morally significant. If I cannot influence my actions, they cannot be deemed either good or bad. If the person accused of a crime argues that he or she is an automaton, totally determined within an overall causal system, then there is no question of guilt about what has happened. On the other hand, the judge passing sentence could argue that the punishment is equally determined, and that he is not free to offer clemency.

In order for anything to be a moral issue, the person concerned has to be exactly that – a 'person'. Machines are not morally responsible, only those who design, manufacture or use them. *No gun has ever been found guilty of murder, only the person who pulled the trigger.*

If morality were to depend only on the physical performance of an action, and intentions were entirely discounted, then goodness and badness would be determined by society and applied to that action regardless of the circumstances. Once the intention of the person becomes significant, and morality becomes a matter of following personally held principles – even to the point of going against society and its rules in order to hold to a more general or deeply held view or commitment – then it is clear that moral praise of blame must assume that the subject is *an autonomous individual*.

There can be pressure, extenuating circumstances and so on, but, ultimately, you have to believe that, for praise of blame, there is a person who sees a situation and responds freely to it, doing what he or she wishes, and therefore reflecting his or her desires, values and intentions. Morality, without individuals who experience themselves as free and intentional, makes no sense.

The point here is that, from a scientific (including a psychological) point of view, everything can be determined by causes outside itself. Every lawbreaker has a reason to break the law, and that reason may be to do with upbringing, values, circumstances and so on. If an action is not completely random (and banks do not get robbed by random passers-by!), then there are reasons for it having taken place.

That said, for those taking part in the game of life, there are choices to be made – choices that lead to moral praise or blame. The experience is of freedom, and with it comes guilt, or self-satisfaction, moral praise or blame. Of course, as Heidegger pointed out (see Chapter ch033), I am 'thrown' into my situation in life, and can never know the totality of the background influences upon me, but that does not stop me from affirming myself. *To give way on the issue of human freedom is to abdicate what is distinctive about being human; to choose to see oneself as an 'object' rather than affirming oneself as a 'subject'.*

Once we touch on ethics, we see how important it is not to adopt a simple identification of the self with neural activity. Just consider some of the following:

▶ If all actions are simply the result of brain activity, then repairing brains rather than punishing individuals is seen as the answer to bad behaviour. If, that is, anyone can decide what 'bad' behaviour is, since 'bad' is normative and not visible to neuroscience.
▶ Sorry, but I think there must have been an overproduction of dopamine which suggested I steal that car and drive it at an

illegally high speed – I just saw the chance of doing it and went for it! I am not to blame; it is entirely the result of too much chemical stimulus.

▶ Our choices are the result of activity in the frontal cortex, our emotions to what is happening in the amygdala; we are but the helpless victims of what is happening in our brains.

▶ If particular neural pathways become faster as you learn or develop new skills, making subsequent activity more efficient, who has responsibility for that training? If the answer is that nobody is responsible for that process – it just happens as a result of external stimulus – then who you become and what skills you acquire depend entirely on circumstances.

▶ Since your brain controls all aspects of your body, and since neurons have no morality, does that imply that moral behaviour is a fiction?

Of course, for strict eliminative materialists morality is a product of evolution and is explicable in terms of neuroscience. It is developed out of basic self-protection mechanisms, extending to include protective concern for offspring and members of the same species. All else is explicable in terms of social convention.

It is difficult to see how such a theory could be *disproved*, since any alternative account of moral dilemmas will simply be assumed to be a product of the same evolutionary process. What we have to ask is whether it appears to give an *adequate* account of our experience of the process of sorting out a moral dilemma, or of establishing principles upon which we wish to act. We could suggest, for instance, that society would work far more efficiently if moral rules were sufficiently hard-wired that moral dilemmas did not occur and we simply got on with our respective tasks, like worker ants. What possible evolutionary advantage could the inefficient process of sorting out moral dilemmas bring to the species?

Well, that question is open to debate, but it is clear that social cooperation and a natural sense of *care* for others underpins morality, and – since *Homo sapiens* has developed more and more complex social and moral environments – it is fair to assume that Darwin was right that social and moral intelligence is a product of natural selection. However, we need to remember that 'is a product of' is not simply to be equated with 'is reducible to'. In other words, seeing social and moral progress in evolutionary terms does not reduce it to a simple physical or mechanical process of computation – both the plasticity of our brains and the complex nature of our social networks and value systems, ensure that the discussion of morality needs to work at a level very different from the measurement of neural activity.

ANIMALS?

There is no doubt that human beings live lives that are very different from those of other species. Language, culture and technology ensure that we are far more complex in our intellectual and emotional lives than other animals – that goes without saying. However, that should not lead us to the unwarranted assumption that human minds are utterly unlike those of other species in terms of their basic functioning.

It is difficult to say at what point we can talk about creatures becoming conscious in the way that human beings are aware of their own consciousness. One of the key tests is an understanding of the experience of pain. Thus it may be considered wrong to inflict pain on an animal. Clearly, an ape can feel pain – since it is expressing enough, and is similar enough in its basic physiology to humans, to be able to convey that. But what about an ant, or an earthworm? If the two halves of the worm severed by my garden spade writhe about, does that indicate pain, or just a natural muscular reaction? The answer is, of course, that we have no means of knowing. We can never know 'what it is like' to be another creature.

However, in examining the functionalist approach to mind, particularly in the context of artificial intelligence, we saw that *multiple realizations* are possible (for example in a brain and in a computer). Now, if that same mental property can be brought about by ('realized in') different physical arrangements, it cannot be identified with any one of them. This may also have implication for our understanding of the personality traits displayed by animals. If an emotion (e.g. friendliness) is expressed functionally, rather than physically, then it might well be realized in similar ways in the different physical make-up of both animals and humans. Of course, not all friendliness is the same (the dog that comes up to lick me may be genetically programmed to do so in a way that I am not), but that can be a difference between human individuals as well as between humans and other species. You may not know why a dog behaves in a particular way, but you probably don't know why I do either!

But if multiple realizations are possible, then it is only prejudice that prevents us from entertaining the idea that what the dog *feels* in terms of happiness, sadness, or the desire to welcome someone familiar may be *exactly the same as I feel*. Just as we find that the same basic elements throughout the universe – water and ice will be the same, even if found on a distant planet – so elements of consciousness need not be limited to the human realm, but may be realized in many different species.

If that is so, then we need to take our treatment of animals seriously. They are not automata, just because we cannot communicate with them as we would with another human being. This is not to give them human characteristics, merely to recognize that they have sensations and emotions that are parallel to ours, and therefore need to be treated with a degree of ethical sensitivity that goes beyond a simple assessment of whether or not they can feel pain.

But whether we are dealing with animals or human beings, the key thing to recognize is that the mind operates at the level of the whole creature, that it is intentional and that it is proactive. If we assume that our understanding of the mind can be entirely handed over to neuroscience, we shall lose all three of those key features. It is also important to recognize – as we saw earlier in looking at the way in which we develop as persons – that we develop through mapping out the world in terms of value and significance. In other words, our exploration of the world is *normative*. This is not just essential for an awareness of morality, it is key to the whole of our understanding of what it is to live and act purposefully as a human being.

10 THINGS TO KEEP IN MIND

1 The key problem for Descartes was how the mind could cause changes in the physical body.

2 The mind cannot be an additional link in a physical causal chain.

3 Human freedom is unlikely to be revealed in terms of neural activity, or at the quantum level.

4 Spinoza thought that freedom was an illusion caused by a failure to know all the causes of our action.

5 Kant considered that we could be both phenomenally conditioned and noumenally free.

6 Intentional states are normative if they are about values.

7 Actions are intentional and instrumental.

8 Personal morality and responsibility require that we do not blame our brain for what we do.

9 We cannot assume that other species do not experience emotions as well as sensations, with implications for their ethical treatment.

10 It is through our intentions and values that we develop as persons.

10

The creative mind

In this chapter you will:
- *consider whether the current debate about mind is too narrowly focused*
- *examine the mind's role in religion and the creative arts*
- *explore a Buddhist perspective.*

The act of writing captures a string of ideas and records them in a way that makes them publicly accessible. There is a direct connection between thought and writing, or thought and speech. Writing is the record of intellectual activity; it makes public and accessible the mental activity that corresponds to (but is not revealed by) neural activity.

The words that I am keying into my computer at this moment are, from a physicalist perspective, totally determined by physical causes – including the firing of neurons in my brain and the resulting instructions to my nerves and finger muscles. They are the product of brain activity that is itself a response to input in terms of experience, including the experience of reading a number of books and listening to other people speak.

But that leaves out of account everything we understand by intellectual creativity. Without my selecting subjects to study, books to read, university courses to attend, the inputs would not have been such as to produce this particular book as their corresponding output. And why should I now be writing about subjects I first studied more than 40 years ago? Why delay the output? The explanation for that lies with a social network that includes publishers, bookshops, the current market for philosophy books, what I've been doing in the intervening years and many other things.

Our experience of creative activity is far removed from language about neural pathways. We cannot deny that a functioning brain is necessary for creative activity, and it would be absurd to attempt to return to a simple and absolute dualism in which the mind is entirely separate from, and only problematically connected to, the brain and the rest of our body. But physicalism cannot have the last word here, for an analysis of physical causality – however beneficial medically and however brilliantly it can probe what is happening in the brain – simply cannot account for the initiation of original thought. If a closed causal sequence defines our every thought and action, we are locked into a fatalistic determinism that belies our experience.

Science often uses a method called 'inference to the best explanation' when deciding between theories. It looks at all possible explanations for a phenomenon and chooses the one that, on the basis of present evidence, seems to be the most likely. It also tends to evaluate a theory in terms of how useful it is, how well it answers earlier problems, and how fruitful it is likely to be in terms of advancing research.

Taking such an approach, we may ask the following question: *Which is the more useful theory to accept as a working basis for understanding the mind – that mental and intellectual activity is real and has a significance beyond the physical, although for any one individual it is physically located in brain activity, or that mental and intellectual activity does not exist, and that everything may be fully explained in terms of neuroscience?*

Clearly, I'm putting the extreme options here, but do so in order to make an important point. We are easily bewitched into thinking that technology will solve fundamental problems. Hence, the ability to observe and measure neural activity appears to give us an answer to the question of how body and mind relate to one another. The truth is that neuroscience has not answered the question posed to Descartes by Princess Elizabeth of Bohemia in 1643. True, it has discouraged us from accepting a straight Cartesian dualism, but only by attempting to eliminate the mind. But the broad sense of her question remains: *How do we explain the way in which we, as human beings, make a difference in this world of physical causality?*

Neuroscience might extend its remit to suggest that 'we' are no more than an illusion, and that it is our brain that controls us. But that view is based on analysis and examination of the mechanisms by which we operate. It does not engage the person as a whole, and it certainly does not take into account the social element in our mental life – that our thoughts and words are shared and take on a life beyond the individual.

Too narrow a view?

The processing and manipulation of data is only purposeful if it seeks to realize pre-established goals. I know if a computer works well because I expect it to perform certain tasks, as stated on the box the software came in. I measure performance against the accomplishment of those tasks and hence the delivery of the goals I require. Part of the problem with using a computer as an analogy for the human process of thinking and consciousness is that it denies the essential element of freedom that characterizes human life. The office worker who assesses his or her life simply on performance across a desk is judged a sad character! The key feature of human consciousness is that it constantly breaks out of the moulds into which others try to fit it.

People only settle into a narrow view of their life's potential out of fear of the scope of their consciousness, and where it might lead them. The existential philosopher, therapist, novelist or playwright is likely to have a better notion of what human consciousness is about than the philosopher studying the possibility of creating artificial intelligence. To someone who attempted to program a computer to compose a Beethoven symphony, in the desperate attempt to understand Beethoven, I would say: 'If you want to understand Beethoven, don't try to reproduce him artificially, go out and listen to (or better, perform in) one of his symphonies!'

Analysis and reconstruction may be useful if one is trying to understand the workings of a crude mechanical device, but it really doesn't work with human consciousness. It assumes far too narrow of view of what the human mind is about.

Perhaps one of the clues to understanding human minds and their workings is to remember to look at those things that are of an appropriate size. If dealing with humans, it is little use remaining focused on the microscopic workings of neurons.

Size matters!

Human beings are extremely complex creatures, and it is important to recognize that their 'selfhood' operates at the holistic level. If you attempt a physical analysis of the brain in order to locate mental operations, you cannot get to the heart of the experience of consciousness – for the neurons are just too small to give a picture of the life of the whole person.

What about all the bacteria that inhabit my mouth and gut? They perform a valuable task in digesting food and so on. But are they part of *me*? Taken at the microscopic level there is much that is happening beneath my skin to which I pay no attention and which, as an individual, I regard as irrelevant. Cells reproduce themselves with no conscious interference on my part. And if their reproduction goes wrong, do I regard the resulting cancer as also part of 'me'? Much of what we are carries on regardless. To what extent is all that microscopic activity 'me'? Is the 'real me' not primarily visible at the point at which I make conscious decisions?

On the cosmic scale, our galaxy is eating a small neighbour, but that does not concern us enough to put us off eating our own lunch. And once we have done so, even with the best of dental hygiene, the bacteria in our mouth will start to have their lunch. Every meal is three meals in one – but only the middle one, of which we are immediately involved and conscious, is of significance for us.

And then there is the matter of social interaction. We do not inhabit a world devoid of other human beings. If we did, most of what makes us an individual would be taken away. We are social creatures, dependent at every moment on the environment that supports us. Isolated from that environment, our life expectancy is scarcely a couple of minutes – or however long we can survive without drawing breath.

There is a real sense in which the question 'Who am I?' has to be answered in terms of different levels. Only within a fairly narrow band of size and complexity will the individual appear. Taken to the microscopic level, I vanish in the hectic activity of millions of individual cells. Taken to the macrocosmic, the human species is little more than an interconnecting network of fine dust grains, spread across the thin film of biosphere, on a tiny planet. Only at the level in which my whole self can perceive and relate to other creatures *at that same level*, do I start to become a self.

Let us be clear about the implications of size for our understanding of mind. Of course, I am host to millions of microbes, all living out their lives within my body. Of course, at every moment, there are cells reproducing, white blood cells cruising around looking for foreign invaders to eat, cells growing and then being told by the body to kill themselves because they are in the wrong place. I am a universe of activity, but most of it is of no direct concern to me.

Insight

And notice that, in order to describe their activity, I have to resort to anthropomorphisms – blood cells only act purposefully, because that it how I interpret their significance.

However, if some of those cells start reproducing wrongly, I am in serious trouble. If a microscopic virus gains a foothold in my body, I will get ill. The different physical levels are therefore far from independent of one another. I cannot exist without all those cells and their activity. But my sentient life – my mind and consciousness – operates only at a holistic level, at which I, as a human being, relate to others, explore my own hopes and fears, and so on.

Equally, the atoms of which I am composed were created billions of years ago. The same substances of which I am composed are found throughout the universe – I am part of that greater reality. I know that the present universe will change; stars come and go, taking planets with them. Galaxies collide. The conditions that enable human beings to survive are very precise and temporary. We are here for a very short while on the surface of this planet, a lucky chance in an inhospitable universe. But, again, that does not generally concern me. My mind does not operate at the universal level, but at the human. True, a stray chunk of cosmic debris could wipe out life on Earth, but that is so beyond my ability to intervene and do anything about it, that I do not take it into consideration.

If we are to consider the nature of mind, it must be at the level at which mind works, and that is neither the cosmic nor the microscopic, but the *personal* and *individual*.

Religion and metaphysics

In the medieval world, fear of eternal damnation and the fate of the soul after death were great religious motivators. That has largely gone, but we might still ask about the broad religious and metaphysical implications of the study of the mind. If the mind really is creative, what does it say about religion or the idea of a life beyond the limits of the physical body?

There are philosophers who give to mind a supremely creative function. One of the most challenging features of the philosophy of Friedrich Nietzsche is his argument that we are called on to shape and mould our own lives very much in the way that an artist sets about creating an image.

This view is by no means new. A key feature of the philosophy of the Buddha in the 6th century BCE is that our life is the creation of our mind, and that every thought we have and every choice we make has a part to play in shaping our future. To understand my present situation, I have to look at my thoughts and choices of yesterday. To know my future, I have to examine my present thoughts and choices. Rather than considering the mind to be some esoteric entity whose relationship to the material world is problematic, the Buddha starts with the experienced reality of mental activity. Our minds are what solve our problems and decide what we should do – they are the shaping force that directs the material body.

From such a perspective, it is nonsense to try grubbing about among the neurons to 'find' the seat of consciousness. The mind is that which, through a constant process of exploring, learning and responding, relates the individual to his or her environment, and takes charge of the many functions that are necessary for life, from controlling breathing, feeling sexually aroused and able to reproduce, finding food and drink, devising means of avoiding excessive heat and cold, and on from these basic needs to the whole web of needs and expectations of modern human society.

Religious and metaphysical ideas have traditionally provided a framework within which experience makes sense to us. They also express the normative – the valuation we give to the things we encounter. As such, they would seem to be a natural extension of the basic intentional and functional understanding of the mind. But once metaphysical or religious beliefs are articulated we hit a problem:

- ▶ The intentional and normative stance tends to produce a framework of ideas and values within which we live and make sense of our experience.
- ▶ If we wish to share that framework or its values, we are forced to use concepts that have an agreed public meaning.
- ▶ Our rational faculties tend to analyse and assess concepts, based on our most basic values and insights.
- ▶ Hence there will always be a tendency to question the validity of any socially established framework of ideas, testing it against our own personal 'map'.

The fact that religions have developed at different times in very different cultures suggests that they are the product of a very basic mental function, mapping out a world of value and significance. On the other hand, since we test out whatever we experience, there will always be a tendency to challenge established metaphysical and religious ideas.

BEYOND DEATH?

We have already touched on ideas of life after death and near-death experiences, but a consideration of the creative nature of mind raises the question as to whether it has a role in seeing the significance of the individual in a way that is not physically limited. The idea of a life that transcends death, either by continuing afterwards in some way, or by belonging to a different realm (the eternal) which is not touched by the changes and final ending of the physical body, is held by a majority of religious people.

Clearly, of the various possibilities in terms of the relationship between the self and the physical body, survival of any sort requires dualism. Those who take a materialist view, or even an epiphenomenal approach to the relationship between body and mind (see Chapter 2), exclude the possibility of life separate from the physical body. Survival requires there to be something beyond the physical.

What might that 'beyond' be? First of all, in a spacetime continuum, time and space are linked; if something is eternal, it must be beyond any limitations of time, and therefore also beyond any limitations of space. In other words, it is logically impossible (given the nature of the universe we live in) to have something which is physically limited and located, but also eternal. If eternal life means anything, it is about the role of the self b*eyond* our individual body or any physical limitations.

That being the case, one might look on the expanding identities of the self, and the way this relates to the eventual dissolution of its physical matrix:

▶ As far as the individual goes, death of the physical body is certain.

▶ For a family or organization, the physical reality goes beyond any one individual.

▶ For a larger group, such as a nation or race, life continues through others who share that nationality or racial group.

▶ For humanity, continuity is more realistic, being limited only by the conditions that prevail on earth being compatible with human existence.

▶ One might go further (as in Buddhism and Jainism) and contemplate unity within all sentient life.

▶ Finally, one feels some sort of identity with the universe as a whole.

Clearly, the perceived life of the self is proportional to the dimensions of the physical reality *with which it is identified*. If the focus is on the human individual, it is always going to prove difficult to argue for a personal and natural immortality, simply because the physical matrix that gives the individual identity is temporary. Only by extending the concept of 'self' outwards to include a wider and wider physical matrix does the extension of the life of that self become more realistic.

Insight

A war hero, deliberately sacrificing himself in the heat of battle, sees himself at that moment as simply part of a larger group – that of his nation. His or her life means something, continues even, through that wider identification. The same would apply to a religious martyr, or those who sacrifice themselves to save friends of family. To die for a cause it to see one's life in that wider context.

Your life is what you identify as your life. If your life is simply what goes on in and around your body, with the wider world there solely to provide what you need – then you are doomed. Your life will end with your body. Those who say 'my family is my life' already acknowledge a sense of life beyond their own death. And so on, until we arrive at the mystic, who is able in some way to identify his or her life with the universe as a whole, and who loses all fear of death. The ending of the body is almost irrelevant, for 'life' (in the sense of what one 'is') has expanded outwards to embrace everything.

Insight

My point is that *the mind thus creates its own awareness of immortality*. It cannot simply 'continue', just as it is, onwards through time – for that would require a permanent but limited physical existence. Rather, it can expand its awareness outwards; creating a sense of self that is progressively freed from its physical origins.

The creative arts

Artistic creativity is a fact of human life and culture, and has been since the earliest cave paintings. It is, of course, closely linked with religious sensitivity – since both religion and the arts seek to express the meaning and significance of life.

In terms of the philosophy of mind, creativity goes against any sense that the mind is a mere epiphenomenon, produced as an accidental and impotent offshoot of brain activity. However intimately it is linked with what happens in the brain, artistic creativity certainly goes beyond any mechanical or predetermined processing of experience. The artist 'sees as' in a variety of ways, and the experience of a work of art can change one's own perception.

The process of musical composition, for example, is one that allows emotions to be encapsulated in a physical form quite unlike that within which were originally encountered, but which is able to ignite those emotions in others. The love of the countryside is not, in itself, a musical experience, yet there is music that can evoke a sense of rural bliss. Similarly with war, or patriotism, or tragic loss – those emotions and experiences are handled and processed (consciously or unconsciously) by the composer, so that they can be evoked in the hearer.

There is, of course, debate between modernism and postmodernism on the role of the creative artist or author. All we need to do here is to be aware that, whether expressing a personal essence or gathering together bits of preformed cultural material, there is a creative role that enables the self to shape and give meaning to physical entities. What the artist produces (like it or hate it) is said to 'mean something' to the artist, or to be a statement about how that artist sees reality.

> **Insight**
> The artistic self is not passive, but active. It does not simply register and respond to external reality, but creates. Any view of the self that does not take artistic creativity into account is inadequate.

A Buddhist perspective

Buddhist philosophy is particularly concerned to explore the nature of the self, since it argues that a limited and fixed idea of self is the root cause of suffering. Indeed, breaking down conventional notions of the self is central to the Buddhist path.

Buddhist philosophy is complex, and reflects the many different cultural traditions embraced by the Buddhist tradition. Nevertheless, there are some basic views of the nature of the self that are part of the earliest tradition, and therefore reflect the approach of a majority of Buddhist thinkers.

Key to Buddhist thinking is the idea that the 'self' is merely a conventional idea, and that ultimately there is no fixed or permanent self. The Buddha suggested that a person is made up of five *skandhas* (or bundles), namely:

▶ **Form** – our physical body, including its sense organs; this is seen as constantly changing and completely dependent upon its material environment.
▶ **Sensations** – including all sense impressions but also ideas (since Buddha regarded the mind as a form of sixth sense, gathering and registering ideas).
▶ **Perceptions** – the mind can only understand the sensations it receives by a process of conceptualization. Perceptions are the 'seeing as' of Western thought.

- **Mental formations** – these are the habitual attitudes and actions that are our response to our sensations and perceptions. They give us our character.
- **Consciousness** – this is the fundamental awareness of being alive and processing all that comes to us through the senses. Each sense is said to have its own distinctive form of consciousness.

The Buddha's view was that each of these five *skandhas* is constantly changing. Nothing is fixed. There is no separate, permanent, eternal 'soul' or self (a teaching known as *anatta*). Buddhism is not a speculative philosophy but more a programme of personal development, with a view to increasing wisdom and compassion. Each teaching therefore has a particular, existential purpose in mind, and practical consequences.

The teaching of *anatta* is designed to avoid the suffering that comes from craving, and the roots of craving are seen in the false notion that we are permanent and fixed, and that the rest of the world is somehow there to provide for us.

The recognition that the self is a flow of experiences, coming into being and passing away in response to circumstances, is seen as a more realistic view of life and a basis for seeing common cause with all other sentient beings.

Insight

It is very difficult to fit the Buddhist view of the self into any of the Western categories. It is certainly not dualistic in a Cartesian sense, nor does it see the mind (or self, since the thinking 'mind' in Buddhist philosophy is almost like an extra sense, over and above sensations, volitions and so on) as merely a by-product of physical activity. Rather, both physical and mental realms are in a state of flux, with entities being distorted as soon as they are fixed conceptually. In other words, as soon as I start to clarify 'my mind' or 'my body' I am already moving away from the ever-changing reality, towards a distorted and distorting notion of permanence.

For our purpose, it is enough to note that, from a Buddhist perspective, the notion of the self is the key to all else – on the grounds that one cannot understand the nature of the world, nor know how to respond to it positively, without a realistic view of the self.

This is very different from Western religion and philosophy, which has tended to start with overall speculation about the nature of things (metaphysics) or the nature of God, and has then developed an idea of the self to fit those existing ideas.

Ironically, it is modern science that has shown the folly of that approach. It recognizes that understanding of the world is always shaped by the ways in which we perceive it: we cannot get a truly 'objective' view of anything. In other words: we understand the world only by means of our own consciousness. Hence, if we do not appreciate how we look at things, we will never understand the things we are seeing.

And sometimes I just sit…

Sometimes you sit and think, and at other times you just sit. Part of the curse of the mind/body issue and many of the problems that arise when considering consciousness, is the fact that (as Hume said) we never experience ourselves except as having some thought or other. The mind is a continuously running kaleidoscope. But need it be?

One of the most creative experiences, explored in many religions, particularly in the East, but also in many self-help and therapy contexts in the West, is the quieting of the mind in meditation

Naturally, it is difficult to explain meditation experiences, since they contain at best rough analogies with other mental states. But a key feature is the immediacy of experience. The breakthrough comes when we no longer think about what we are doing in meditation, but just enter into the experience itself. At that moment, the question 'Who am I?' becomes irrelevant. The very notion of defining the self – and thereby distinguishing the self from everything that is 'not self' seems superficial and pointless.

In many ways (as mystics have claimed from all religious traditions), the self/world distinction can be transcended, we can be aware of ourselves as being part of a universal reality, focused in a particular time and place. Indeed, accounts of meditation or mystical experience suggest that there can be an expanded sense of the self for which its particular physical matrix seems almost irrelevant.

> To be lost in music, enraptured by a work of art, absorbed in a creative activity – all these approach the same experience that is explored through meditation. It is an utter excentration of the self, turning it inside out, so that personal meaning is now experienced as much on the outside as on the inside.

Heidegger criticized his former mentor Husserl for not properly breaking free from the self/world dualism of Descartes, and therefore for continuing to see our relationship with the world as primarily one of observer and observed and as taking an intentional stance towards it. By contrast, Heidegger saw our primary way of being in the world as that of engagement. We are there, thrown into a particular situation, living in a way that is always aware of our finiteness, finding and using the things that come to our hand. For him, the division between subjective self and objective world is a secondary reflection; far more basic are the existential concerns and commitments that shape our life. In our ordinary, everyday activity we are at home in the world, getting on with things, using tools, sorting the things that are around us. Only when we stop and reflect do we become aware of the subject/object division.

Hence we do not need to sit in meditation to overcome the dualism of self and world, with its accompanying problems of mind and body, there is another route – that of engaged activity. When absorbed in activity, we are fully ourselves but also fully within physical situation. And that applies to the child absorbed in a game as much as a Zen master engaging in calligraphy.

Experiencing that undifferentiated state – whether through the arts, or meditation, or religion – does not necessarily provide answers to all the questions we have set out in this book, but is more likely to suggest to us that, for the most part, *we do not need to ask them.*

10 THINGS TO KEEP IN MIND

1 Creativity is social and cannot be adequately accounted for in terms of brain function.

2 The question of self-identity needs to be asked at the appropriate level – namely that of the individual.

3 Religion, as a phenomenon, relates to the normative and mapping functions of the mind.

4 The significance of one's own death depends on the scope of one's self-identification.

5 The creative arts 'see as' and express mental content.

6 In Buddhism, the self is seen as a bundle of five skandhas.

7 Buddha considered the idea of a fixed and permanent self to be the cause of suffering.

8 Meditation and the arts can promote immediate experience that transcends subject/object awareness.

9 Heidegger saw engagement as prior to the perceived division between self and world.

Postscript: Of maps and pathways

Clearly, the central question for the philosophy of mind today concerns the relationship between the whole range of things that we associate with the mind – from simple consciousness to cultural creativity – and neuroscience. And that, as we have seen, has highlighted rather than answered the double-sided question that has dominated the mind/body debate since Descartes: *How can it be that the mind can made a difference in the physical world, or that a physical brain can produce the experience of consciousness and mind?*

To give you my personal view on this, I want to highlight two images:

1 In looking at the way in which we develop as persons, we explored the idea that we each construct a personal map, spread over our experienced world, on which – overlay by overlay – our memory marks out our experience of value and meaning. In every waking moment, we see the world mapped out before us. Our consciousness is not of raw data, but of experiences that are shaped and given meaning and value by our whole personal history. We are not impersonal recording devices, but personal interpreters of experience. Everything I see I immediately relate to my map. I like one thing and dislike another because of my past experiences. Our identity is established by our map.

2 Now consider the role of neural pathways. We know that the brain is plastic and its neural structures are constantly being reshaped. The billions of connections between neurons form pathways responding to experience. Those we use regularly we strengthen; those we neglect become severed. In this way the brain is responding to life, becoming attuned to our needs. As we go through life, our neural pathways express who we are. This is not in any way to trivialize the complexity of the functioning brain, nor to deny that its different parts have different functions and so on. But everything that neuroscience shows now – whether it is our ability to learn a new skill, or the way in which, following a stroke, other parts of the brain attempt to take over

the function of the part that is damaged – points to the essential plasticity that makes the brain so very different from our fast but relatively crude computers.

I suggest that it is no coincidence that these two images, the one reflecting our personal engagement with the world and the other the workings of our brain, show a remarkable similarity. The constant reshaping and directing of neural pathways in response to experience is what we experience by the process of learning and valuing our world. But if what neuroscience tells us about the brain's plasticity is correct, then the implication is that we shape our brains as much as our brains shape us. The mind cannot be a simple epiphenomenon of brain activity, because it is what we term 'mind' – including that broader sense of linguistic and cultural engagement – that shapes experience, which in turn is mapped out within the brain.

How might this confluence of map and pathways be expressed in terms of the traditional mind/body options? None, it seems to me, is fully adequate; but of those on offer, the closest match comes with something like a dualism of properties, a double-aspect theory, or a non-reductive materialism.

There cannot be a simple subject/object divide here. After all, neuroscience itself is an activity carried out by human minds; the physical object is only understood through the engaged subject. But, just because our mapping of the world is *experienced* whereas our neural pathways are *observed*, does not imply that either of them can be properly understood if the other is left out of account.

Of course, some might argue that this begs the question of how exactly our brains cause our sensations, since analysis of neural functioning cannot show 'what it is like' to be us. But I would argue that it is a bogus question. To suggest that we should be able to explain the production of subjective consciousness scientifically implies that there is a single causal chain that embraces both the physical and the mental. But we have surely had enough consideration of Descartes' pineal gland or Ryle's category mistake to recognize the folly of trying to get that a single causal chain across 'Leibniz's gap'! No perfect neuroscience can answer that question because neuroscience itself is the product of minds.

On 1 February 2012, the day I finished revising the new edition of this book, I turned on the radio to hear the news that neuroscience had apparently made yet another breakthrough. It had become possible to reproduce the internal dialogue of an unconscious person. The result sounded rather rough, and had the date been 1 April I would have thought it a hoax, but there it was. Should we all gasp and change our views of the mind/body relationship on account of this? Of course not. It reinforces our conclusion that the neural pathways and the mapping out of our lives, including the language we use, are two sides of the same coin. Why is it not perfectly reasonable that the neural pathways of my silent, inner monologue of thought should not be exactly those that I would also use to articulate those thoughts? Perhaps this is a step nearer to that perfect neuroscience that eliminative materialists assume will render the mind irrelevant. But when that day arrives, I sense that we shall see exactly what has been staring us in the face all along, that the mind of an individual is made possible by, and is physically located in, the brain, while its experienced significance is not neural but personal, social and cultural.

Our neural pathways and the maps through which we understand our world and our selves *are two complementary aspects of the functioning of a human being*. The complexity of the former makes possible the wonderful richness of the latter. Nothing less than billions of neural connections can provide the mechanism capable of embodying the experience of being human.

Glossary

behaviourism The view that mental attributes apply to physical behaviour.

cognitive science The general term for the range of disciplines which (since the 1970s) work together in considering the nature of human cognition (knowledge).

consciousness A general term with a variety of meanings, including a being's awareness of and response to the environment, and also its self-awareness.

double-aspect theory The view that all reality has both physical and mental aspects.

dualism The view that there are two kinds of substance: physical substance, which has extension and location, and is the object of scientific study; and mental substance, which is not physically located, and comprises our thoughts and conscious states. There is also **property dualism** and **concept dualism**, which distinguish mind and body, but without requiring mind to have a separate substance.

eliminative materialism The view that mental phenomena do not exist as such, and that a perfect neurobiology would explain all there is to know about the mind.

epiphenomenalism The idea that mind is a generated as a result of brain activity, but cannot itself determine brain activity.

externalism The view that mental content is 'about' external things, and therefore only makes sense in shared environments, where it may be described using shared language.

functionalism The view that the mind has a functional role in assessing inputs from the senses and giving the appropriate responses. Mental states are not identified with physical states, but the mental does not exist apart from the physical.

idealism The view that there is only one kind of substance, the mental (the physical world we encounter is, in fact, only known in terms of the mental awareness we have of it).

intentionality The view that all consciousness is directed towards some object, and that all thought is therefore 'about' something.

materialism (or physicalism) The view that there is only one kind of substance, the physical.

occasionalism The theory that mental sensations occur on the occasion of their corresponding physical occurrences, but are not directly caused by them.

phenomenological fallacy The error of assuming that experienced phenomena are descriptions of internal brain states.

pre-established harmony The view that the mental and physical universes are independent, but designed by God to work together in harmony

privileged access The view, from a dualist perspective, that each individual has a unique access to his or her own mind.

qualia the phenomenological qualities of experience (i.e. the experience of something as having a particular colour, texture, sound, etc.).

skandhas Buddhist term for the 'bundles' of which the self is comprised.

solipsism The view that we can have no certain knowledge of other minds, and are therefore alone in our world.

structuralism An early theory of psychology, which attempted to understand the structure of the mind through the analysis and recording of the phenomena of experience.

supervenience The view that mental properties overlay, rather than replace, physical ones.

Further reading

The literature on the philosophy of mind is huge. The following represent no more than a limited and personal selection of books that I have found to be particularly helpful.

For a substantial anthology of texts in this area, try *Mind and Cognition*, ed. William Lycan, in the Blackwell Philosophy Anthologies (2nd edn, Blackwell, 1999).

The Nature of Mind, ed. David M. Rosenthal (Oxford University Press, 1991) is an older anthology, but clearly set out and covering the essential ground for students.

The Oxford Handbook of Philosophy of Mind, ed. Brian McLaughlin, Ansgar Beckermann and Sven Walter (Oxford University Press, 2009) brings together 45 contributions, covering every aspect of the subject.

A good summary of the traditional issues, along with a critical assessment of cognitive science, artificial intelligence and functionalism, can be found in John Searle, *The Rediscovery of Mind* (MIT Press, 1992). This book is very clear, hard-hitting and readable.

Or try Jaegwon Kim, *Philosophy of Mind* (Westminster Press, 1996) or John Heil, *The Philosophy of Mind* (Oxford University Press, 2004).

Also from MIT Press (Massachusetts Institute of Technology) is *The Philosophy of Mind: Classical Problems / Contemporary Issues*, ed. B. Beakey and P. Ludlow (1992), an anthology of readings from ancient Greece to the present day, giving a fine historical overview of the subject.

Contemporary Debates in Philosophy of Mind, ed. Brian McLaughlin and Jonathan Cohen (Blackwell, 2007) covers three main areas: mental content, physicalism and the place of consciousness in nature. There are some detailed arguments here, requiring careful attention and background knowledge.

On the limitations of a naturalistic understanding of the human person and the social nature of emotions and meanings, see Charles

Taylor, *Philosophy and the Human Sciences* (Cambridge University Press, 1996).

On artificial intelligence, and for a review of the development of cognitive science, see *Minds, Brains and Computers*, ed. R. Cummins and D.D. Cummins (Blackwell, 2000).

For a theological and biblical perspective on this, particularly concerned with morality, reductionism and free will, see Nancy Murphy, *Bodies and Souls, or Spiritual Bodies?* (Cambridge University Press, 2006). Murphy argues that it is possible to take a generally physicalist position while doing justice to the religious perspective.

David Chalmers, *The Conscious Mind* (Oxford University Press, 1996) is an important contribution from an influential philosopher in this area. Not exactly an easy read, but presents a clearly argued alternative to a reductionist approach.

For minds in other species, and the role of language in the development of the human mind, see Daniel Dennett's *Kinds of Minds* (Weidenfeld & Nicholson, 1996). His other books include *Darwin's Dangerous Idea* and *Consciousness Explained*.

For a work that takes dualism seriously, although written from a basically physicalist position, see Peter Carruthers, *The Nature of the Mind* (Routledge, 2004).

For a wonderfully engaging exploration of the nature of the self, see Julian Baggini, *The Ego Trick* (Granta, 2011).

For an assessment of the scope of what neuroscience can and cannot show, and a campaign against simplistic reductionism, see Raymond Tallis, *Aping Mankind* (Acumen, 2011).

And, finally, for an exploration of how we construct and maintain our personal identity, try Mel Thompson, *Me* (Acumen, 2009).

For further information about books and Internet resources on the philosophy of mind, notes for students and his other books on philosophy, religion and ethics, visit the author's website: mel-thompson.co.uk

Index